THE WHOLESCHOOL BOOK

teaching and learning late in the 20th century

bob samples
cheryl charles
dick barnhart

Addison-Wesley Publishing Company
Reading, Massachusetts
Menlo Park, California ● London ● Amsterdam ● Don Mills, Ontario ● Sydney

All photos and graphics by Bob Samples, Cheryl Charles, Olina Gilbert, Dick Barnhart and Dick Gilbert.

ISBN 0-201-06699-8
ABCDEFGHIJ-HA-7987

Jordi L. Brinton

Preface

This book is about teaching and learning. Unlike most books about these subjects *THE WHOLESCHOOL BOOK* focuses on the teacher.

It is clear that good, enriching education can occur anywhere, anytime, and under abysmal circumstances. But if it does . . . it is always traceable to a competent teacher . . . a person whose psyche is in good shape and whose ego strength can withstand almost any circumstance.

It has been popular to think that great teachers are born and not made. In our experience, this is not entirely true. Good teachers are those who want to teach, who care about themselves and care about students. They are flexible, competent and have a good sense of humor. This book focuses on how each of these qualities can be nurtured and celebrated.

Teaching can be a routine, a punishment or a technology. *Or* it can become a transformative way of experiencing life . . . for *both* the teacher and the students. *THE WHOLESCHOOL BOOK* treats this last possibility. We do not pretend to know *the* way. But in these pages we share a variety of ways that have grown out of a collective experience of hundreds of teachers and tens of thousands of students.

If anything, *THE WHOLESCHOOL BOOK* is a human experience. There is no glossing over the harsher realities of education. Platitudes about the classroom experience are hard to find in these pages. But there are words of hope . . . because we do believe in the power and strength of human decency. In short, good people are good teachers. In the classroom and in life, good teachers are transformed as much as they transform. They live life in ways that insure each day, each week, and each year are new periods of growth.

To

Betty Joy
Jim Gladson
Barbara Yamamoto
Dick Konicek
Frank Watson
Ken Peterson
Jake Nice
and
Michele Hensill
who are out there doin' it!

Introduction

This is a book for teachers and for learners. We would like there to be no necessary difference between the two. One can be a teacher *and* learn. One can be a learner *and* teach. One can enjoy being both.

This is a book about you . . . your students and your setting. It contains a lot of things . . . ideas . . . explorations . . . explanations . . . excuses . . . exaggerations and facts. Unlike many books about teaching, our approach is intended to be personal rather than technical. We care primarily about how a person can be prepared to cope and grow in teaching a math lesson that is interrupted by two announcements, a child sharpening a pencil on the eraser end, and a queasy student throwing up in the aisle of the third row. We care first about that. Because teaching is a human activity.

Teaching is *not* a technology. Surely all things we do can be improved and made more perfect. But these pages will celebrate you as people and not as technicians. We are more concerned with the human method than we are about how closely anyone's actions follow any specific learning theory. It is true that nearly all we claim in this book is based on research . . . but you will not find us defending the research. Rather we will focus on how the acts of teaching and learning are extended into realms of experience that elevate and celebrate the human condition.

Celebrate is a word used often in this book. This word comes from our commitment to a belief in the goodness of people. Far too much of education is oriented toward problems . . . toward things the learner is supposedly doing wrong. We will spend as much if not more time focusing on what the learner is doing *right*. And that includes what the teacher as a learner is doing right.

You are a teacher and you are a learner. You are a person who possesses power. That power exists in your adultness, your role in society, and your expertise. As hard as you try, you cannot erase that power advantage to make the students feel more equal or less affected. Your choice is how that power is to be used.

Throughout this book we will emphasize alternatives and choices. And we will emphasize these choices within the very personal context of the unique human being that you are. However, because we are not actually within your presence unless by some cosmic trick . . . only our words are . . . *you* will have to make the last connection.

Table of Contents

PREFACE   I   INTRODUCTION   III   TABLE OF CONTENTS   IV

THE JOURNEY

Chapter 1	Mind Meadows	1
	Exploring the dominant ways of thinking.	
Chapter 2	Together in the Meadows	12
	Greeting the ways of thinking in self and in students.	
Chapter 3	Meadow Masters	22
	The major schools of thought regarding learning.	
Chapter 4	A Mighty River Flows	46
	The brain, thinking and education.	
Chapter 5	Meadow Paths	55
	Translating theory into classroom practice.	
Chapter 6	Personal Meadows	72
	Reflecting on one's self and teaching.	

PLACES ALONG THE WAY

Chapter 7	The System	86
	How schools work.	
Chapter 8	The Building	100
	Characteristics of the place called school.	
Chapter 9	The Room	112
	The site of learning.	

WEEDS, SEEDS AND GARDENS

Chapter 10   Weeds and Other Living Things   138
             A variety of unexpected realities.

Chapter 11   Gardens of Culture   165
             The role of cultural history and models of instruction.

Chapter 12   Seeds and Germination   182
             Activities for educating the whole child.

VISIONS, DREAMS AND OTHER REALITIES

Chapter 13   Personal Harvests   214
             The mental health of the teacher.

Chapter 14   Meadows of Love   240
             The contexts of love which emerge from teaching and
             learning.

Chapter 15   Seasons of Synergy   250
             The interdependence of all things.

NOTES TO ME   262   GLOSSARY   264   RESOURCES   267

INDEX   270   THANKS   276

The Journey

Mind Meadows

The meadows of mind are unbelievably *personal* places. Whenever any of us are invited to share our minds, a whole universe of events comes rushing into action. Most often only a small fraction of what really takes place in any human mind surfaces in the form of words, sentences, facial expressions, body postures, and other kinds of things we can see and hear.

Inside the brain itself, each thought calls into action a network of neurons and brain cells far greater than the total number of words a human will say in a lifetime! In our thought patterns there are well-established corridors of logic and linearity. They are explored each time words are found to convey our thoughts in meaningful sentences. But these words are chosen against great tapestries of feeling and emotion drawn from a lifetime of experiences. With lightning speed, the threads of these tapestries blend and overlap. With every question we are asked, each of us may feel quick surges of concern as we decide how much to reveal about ourselves. At the same time, we may feel concern for the person who asks the question and try to judge how much he or she can handle.

In school, teachers often give ASSIGNMENTS. An ASSIGNMENT is like a gust of wind across the meadows of mind. It whips the grasses, leaves, insects, and trees. It ruffles the feathers of birds and stirs the fur of animals. It calls a whole ecology into being.

1

Suzie Swain
March 3

The Hallways of Fear

It was dark and the wind was blowing across the top of the grass, now dried and brittle in the autumn chill. Leaves not yet swept away tumbled over the ground like parched sea bats.

The clock ticked steadily toward midnight. My brother and I sat huddled in the dark, peering out of the window into the Halloween night. We shivered in silent anticipation, looking at each other and smothering the giggles that threatened to intrude.

Then we saw it!

It was huge and dark and was moving just beyond the hedge that separated the lawn from the garden. There was a steady, ominous purpose to its motion. We both felt a

2

Education — and its most identifiable parts, teaching and learning — is a beautifully complex thing. It is a dance, a drama, a poem, a tragedy, and a comedy all at once. It is the arena of the "three R's," reading, 'riting, and 'rithmetic. Implicitly, it is the arena of the biggest "R" of all, *rationality*. The "three R's," with their tidiness, terseness, and obedience to rules, are well known to education. To many, they are *the basics* . . . the only purpose for schooling. Susan on the previous page has mastered two and likely three of the "R's." She has carried out the assignment with impact, style, and apparent ease. Most educators would feel she was "together," as the crafts they typically respect are well delivered by Susan. Because she handles these skills with such ease, Susan will often be the model student for her teachers. Many of her teachers will look for other "Susans" as they greet each new group of students. She will set standards for each of her classmates and for most of the rest of the students who come each year into the presence of her teachers. Susan is an ideal student.

But "Is that all there is?" cries the line from the song. We don't think so. Whether sought or not, more than the "three R's" live in the classroom. Raucous, risky, and capricious forces live there as well. They move in casual, sometimes tactless, ways. They are characterized by skills that are difficult to identify. When these forces are expressed, there is so much unpredictability that they are often identified as elements of disorder. But something about these skills "makes sense." We frequently refer to these uncommon skills as "common sense." In urban settings, these skills are often called "street smart." When the forces accompanying these skills prevail, the human mind is operating in ways far different and in some instances more complex than the routines of rationality alone. Emotions, including fears, frustration, timidity, and courage, all blend at once with dozens of other human capacities. Images jumble and juxtapose. Serendipity is celebrated. And intuition is *real*.

The richness of this unpredictable kind of mindwork is often so overwhelming that it cannot be communicated by standard means. Reading, writing, and arithmetic pale, being insufficient to transmit *all* there is.

It is difficult for us to know what Susan really "sensed" that Halloween night. Her use of written language as a tool is so graceful that each of us might easily presume that she felt exactly what she wrote. Susan fits. She does her work so well, a teacher may never look beyond what she produces to see who she is and what else she might be able to do and feel. But the world is not made solely of Susans. In fact . . . meet LEROY.

M'GOD . . . THE TIME I WAS MOST FRIGHTENED WAS WHEN THOSE GUYS STARTED TO HASSLE MY SISTER. I KNEW WHAT THEY WERE UP TO BUT I WAS TOO SMALL . . . THEY HIT ME . . . TASTED LIKE ICE AND KEROSENE . . . I FELT THE LOOSE TEETH . . . AND THEY WERE STEPPIN' ON ME AND I COULD HEAR HER SCREAM-IN' LIKE I NEVER HEARD HER SCREAM. AWFUL . . . KIND OF ANIMAL NOISES. THEY GOT ALL AFTER HER AND FORGOT ME . . . I PICKED UP THE BOARD . . . IT HAD PLASTER AND NAILS IN IT . . . THE FIRST GUY DIDN'T MOVE AFTER I HIT HIM AN' THE PLASTER SPRAYED OFF LIKE WATER. HE BLED A LOT AND I GOT ANOTHER ONE BEFORE THEY NOTICED ME. MY SISTER STOPPED SCREAMIN' AN' WAS REALLY KICKIN' AN' I KNEW SHE WAS OKAY . . . THEY TURNED AT ME AN' ONE GUY GOT A KNIFE OUT. MY SISTER BIT HIS ARM . . . I REMEMBER HER NOSE WAS BLEEDIN' AN' THEN HIS ARM STARTED BLEEDIN' — I GOT ALL COLD INSIDE AN' HIT ANOTHER GUY BEFORE WE HEARD THE SHOT. I COULD SMELL THE POWDER — I WAS SURE THEY KILLED ME BUT IT WAS THE COPS. MY SISTER GRABBED ME AND WE HELD EACH OTHER AN' WAS LAUGHIN' AN' CRYIN' AND THE COPS CAUGHT ONE GUY AN' LOOKED

On the previous page, Leroy's mind, stimulated by an incredibly innocent assignment, returned to thoughts that had never left his preconscious. They hung about his mind like a dream unfulfilled — webbing his conscious thoughts with ghosts of awareness that showed up any time . . . in the halls, on the playground, and in the streets if he saw a gathering of larger boys. The assignment was probably devised by a teacher whose mindset was on far less painful visions of fear. The teacher in all likelihood expected a Halloween episode like Susan's or someone's brother leaping unexpectedly from a hall closet.

Leroy did not conform. His experiences on the streets of a large city led him into many arenas of fear. However, they also led him into arenas of joy. If the assignment had been to describe a "joyful" experience, he could have told about 125th and Lennox on a summer night when all the people were on the stoops . . . "jivin' an' there was music in the hot wind shufflin' the thick sycamores . . . ." But that wasn't the assignment. Further, Leroy made a lot of decisions about how much the teacher could bear. No mention of the details of the violence . . . that he had nearly killed one of the attackers . . . or that his sister barely avoided rape. Leroy offered none of that. His awkward run-on sentence gave us only a superficial glimpse of what might have been more than a run-of-the-mill playground minitragedy.

Analysis of a Complete act of Thought
(paraphrased)

1. Perplexity and Confusion
   (the recognition of a Problem)
2. Tentative Interpretation
   (conjectural anticipation)
3. Careful Survey of Data
   (explorational analysis)
4. Refinement of tentative Hypothesis
5. Testing of the Hypothesis

In 1938 John Dewey — destined to be the major philosopher of education produced in this nation — wrote a small book titled *Logic: A Theory of Inquiry.* In this book, Dewey created a mindset that the culture quickly accepted. In a complicated and second-hand way, this mindset helped prevent Leroy from giving us the full story. In the book, Dewey wrote a section called "The Analysis of a Complete Act of Thought." It is reproduced on this page. Dewey got into the notion that if a mind were logical, thinking would follow the process he described. Later on, educators picked up Dewey's idea and called it "the scientific method."

Percy Bridgeman, a Nobel laureate physicist, years later said that though such a sequence of logic could be determined in regard to the scientific method, he would add more. He said the scientific method is primarily "doing your damnedest with no holds barred." It is likely that Leroy would have liked Bridgeman's extension of the notion much better than Dewey's description. Susan might well have preferred Dewey's.

But Leroy's preferences don't matter much. Somehow logic and "things that make sense" in linear ways dominate the educational setting. Because they do, I as a teacher might be more concerned with the structure, form, and logic of Leroy's response to the assignment than with how Leroy's mind really worked. Susan would not be a problem. In fact, I might well celebrate her as a model.

Leroy favors the realm of "common sense." In his now classic work, Dewey indicated that there is no real difference between logic and common sense. He suggested they differ only in degree. Logic has rules. It is formal. It has grammar, syntax, and an appropriate rhythm. And common sense? Leroy's judgments about the teacher's ability to cope, his choice not to make statements about the near defilement of his sister, and his understatement of his near murder of another human being are all lost . . . in a nongrammatical, dull, run-on sentence.

One of the games that human minds play on themselves is to engage in the belief that all human beings are the same. That because we are supposedly members of the same culture, we are all basically the same. Nothing could be farther from the truth. Each human is a universe — a unique blend of experiences, capabilities, and aspirations. Any strategy used by any of us that treats humans as though they learn, teach, and believe in the same ways is trivial. Such strategies are destined to live a short life — because *they are better at exclusion than at inclusion.* I.Q. tests, achievement tests, and personality inventories are all useful as exercises, and they do tell us something about the people who take them (as well as something about ourselves for giving them). But they are monstrously limited in what they tell us about people. Using such things as more than a basis for conversation is similar to judging the Rocky Mountains on the basis of a pebble picked up in a streambed.

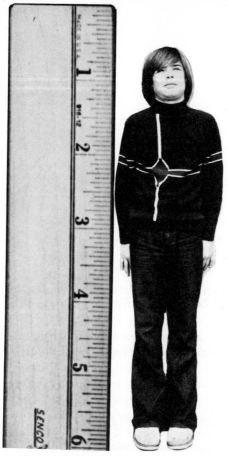

The myth of objectivity is one of the more prevailing myths of our culture. Humans pretend they can judge one another objectively and then proceed to try to do so. The result is that a ghost portrait of the person being judged emerges. The person being judged is ranked, labeled, ability-grouped, and placed in specially designated tracks. Scientists who experiment with the physical universe have known for a long time that there are levels of uncertainty beyond which absolute objectivity is impossible. Atoms, stars, and electronic circuits can never be described with total objectivity. As a result, scientists have had to resort to probability descriptions. Probability descriptions are communicated through statistics. Statistical descriptions can be probability statements only if they are used for prediction . . . and yet they are often used to describe the kind of experience a child will have in school. It is as if students could be described with total objectivity . . . *and they can't!*

Teachers know this well. All over the nation there are cries for accountability. And school districts are demanding that teachers be judged by objective criteria. The response has been both revealing *and* amusing. If the teachers' groups do not rebel outright to the action, they legislate trivial criteria so that there is no way to fail.

Activities

Prove any three of the following:
— birds eat seeds
— seeds eat birds
— blue-eyed girls like rock-climbing better than brown-eyed girls like rock-climbing
— spaghetti eaters are more intelligent than anyone else

Probability and Prediction
— List ten things that will probably happen today.
● Determine as precisely as you can *when* they will happen.
— List the things that can be precisely predicted in terms of the time they will happen.
● Choose which of these things are important to teaching and learning.
— Make a list of ten things you hope will never be predicted.
— Is prediction natural or cultural?

Knowledge
— What is the difference between natural knowledge and cultural knowledge?
— Prove you are knowing while you are sleeping.

Note: Try to find out about the Pygmalion studies.

It is no secret that humans make mistakes. We may well have made a mistake by choosing the examples we did to begin our exploration of the subjects of teaching and learning. A cheap shot? Why Susan Spotless? Why a minority youth? Why a scene of violence?

There is no real way to answer, no real way to explain. We are simply talking about *what happens*. The message, drawn from our experiences in Harlem, is as real in Crown Point, New Mexico; Amherst, Massachusetts; and Sacramento, California, as it is in some form in your community.

Human minds operate far more like cycles of nature than like computers. It is so easy — as each of us preparing to be teachers goes through the highly rational experience of getting a degree in college — to forget a whole arena of mind function that helps to keep us alive. Part of it is that function Dewey called "common sense." Leroy would have called what he knew of it "street smart." We referred to it earlier in these pages as being different from the "three R's." Later on in this book, we will describe its facets in more detail and will call it *metaphoric mind function*.

If you are a beginning teacher, one with ten years' experience, or even one who hasn't started student teaching yet — you still possess that awesome cathedral of humanity and life called "mind." You possess capacities of reason *and* intuition, logic *and* common sense, line *and* metaphor. And so do each of the humans you will touch in your teaching career. So too do each of their parents, their friends, and all of the administrators, counselors, consultants, bus drivers, parents, secretaries, and custodians you will find as you explore the meadows of teaching and learning. These capacities are possessed by all, and yet each human being is different. Each has special qualities and characteristics. Each is unique.

Whatever our uniqueness, most of us interested in teaching and learning spend time — usually a lot of time — in an environment commonly called "school." Schools too are diverse, with emotional, political, intellectual, cultural, and spiritual qualities. That is not to say that such diversity is not to be desired. We celebrate it. Just as we celebrate the differences among human beings. Unfortunately, many schools, just like most of society, are not designed to celebrate or cope effectively with these differences.

Teaching is agony if you assume that all students are the same. It is agony if you assume that all students have the same motivations, the same interests, the same abilities, and the same styles of learning at any moment. Teaching can be a source of joy and learning for all if you accept that each student is different from each of the others. Perhaps it is in the reality of those differences that we find commonality.

10

the joy of life
is in living —
living is partly
school.
All who have joined
in the enterprise
are alive !
Our celebrations have started
at different times...
And are stepped to different
cadences...;
But we are all part.

11

2 Together

in the Meadow

The way school works is the way life is lived. Most of us think we can plan, organize, and carry out a course of action with smoothness and grace. And yet how many of us do? And particularly in the context of the school classroom, where so many variables operate simultaneously, many of which a teacher has little control over. In school classrooms, for example, the best of lesson plans cannot take each child into consideration at every moment. In fact, there is no way that we as authors have any notion where you, the reader of this, might be right now as you read this — not intellectually, emotionally, spiritually, even physically! We know nothing of your experience, your aspirations, your fears, loves, and certainly not of your preferences in Italian food. Oh, we could pretend that we do. Our publishers, editors, and the faculty members and administrators who choose this book for use with you if you happen to be in a pre-service or in-service situation can pretend to know where you are. But none of us do. You might say that our comparison isn't fair . . . because at least teachers with students can see them. You as a teacher, for example, can be with your students in a classroom situation over a period of time and get to know them. There is some truth to that assertion . . . but only some.

Each of you and each of your students has some or all of the qualities of the images on the opposite page. If we were your teacher, we would have to expose ourselves to you, listen to you, and be fully with you in a 181-day drama of honesty before we could pretend any kind of knowing intimacy. We are not saying that kind of intimacy is essential for effective teaching. We are cautioning against the blind webs of assumptions concerning student motivations and abilities that each of us as teachers can easily entangle about us . . . and our students.

To illustrate, we will go further with the example of lesson plans. Because there is such divergence in each classroom and because each child is so different, lesson plans cannot take into account the child who will get a nosebleed or the one who will begin to cry hysterically because her cat was run over. The lesson plans will not be able to accommodate to your feelings . . . whether or not you feel good or are unsettled. The dozens of interruptions which mark each school day are made up of the stubborn fiber of overlapping systems of wants. You will want certain things — and so will the students. Parents, administrators, and other teachers and students too will be a part of the scenario of wants — and of interruptions. And so will the custodian.

We are not intending to say that teaching cannot be done . . . or that it is not a phenomenally rewarding profession. We *are* saying that *effective teaching requires flexibility* and *competence in one's field*. It also requires *a good sense of humor*. History has unfortunately borne out the awareness that competence in one's field generally tends to create an attitude toward structure rather than toward flexibility . . . and toward seriousness rather than humor. This remains true in most human beings until a sense of personal insecurity is lost. When insecurity is lost and true competence is achieved, a kind of psychic relaxation follows. *Flexibility and humor are necessary characteristics of the competent teacher.* Remember, a Susan *and* a Leroy will end up in every class you teach!

flexibility
competence
and a
sense of
humor ?

15

A long time ago, researchers were able to identify certain characteristics of a wide variety of personality types (more will be said about these personality types in the section of the book, *Personal Harvests*). Among the criteria they used were rigidity and flexibility. It was determined very early that traits of rigidity and flexibility were found in remarkably different personalities. Rigidity was a characteristic of people typified by a strong sense of dogma, unyielding values, and an entrenched suspicion of anyone who did not believe in exactly their way. These people — often what we call Authoritarian — were true believers in their own motives. They tended to judge others on the basis of those values they used in their own lives. Milton Rokeach even found out that they tended to lock things up in a compulsive way — their cars, doors, microscope cabinets ... everything. One might imagine that if these people were to keep diaries, they would be the kind with the little locks on them. These people tended also to *think* with locks on their cabinets. When their routines were interrupted, they felt chaos.

Because these people tend to believe that the plan or vision they have is perfect, they seldom see any reason for and thus do not create any alternatives. When something unexpected occurs, they either reject it . . . or overwhelm it. In other words, the unexpected is ignored with the hope that it will go away, or it is aggressively attacked. Teachers with such rigid personalities who also find themselves in agreement with the dominant cultural standards will find Leroy a kind of interruption. Susan is more typically their ideal. They might well label Leroy a "loser" and, with minimum input, ignore him for the rest of the year. Susan, who fits, would be encouraged, nurtured, and carefully tended to. But in a way, *both* students might be losers. Leroy, because he was abandoned by the process of education. And Susan, because she was ingested into it.

The same research studies show another kind of personality that is also highly rigid — but in *conflict* with standard cultural norms. This person is what we call an Antiauthoritarian. Such a person might well choose to celebrate Leroy, while putting Susan down as a "goody-two-shoes." In either case, with the Authoritarian or the Antiauthoritarian, the treachery of rigidity should be obvious. In the presence of such rigidity, someone always loses. Susan and Leroy are *both* humans. Neither deserves or wants to be treated as a category. Each has to want more from life than to be a pawn on someone else's gameboard of rigid expectations.

"It's like the gourmet . . . who gave up everything, traveled thousands of miles and spent his last dime to get to the highest lamasery in the Himalayas to taste the dish he'd longed for his whole life, Tibetan peach pie. When he got there, frostbitten, exhausted and ruined, the lamas said they were all out of peach. 'Okay,' said the gourmet, 'make it apple.' "*

*from *Even Cowgirls Get the Blues* by Tom Robbins. Houghton Mifflin Company, Boston, 1976.

People with *flexible* personalities, on the other hand, were *not* found to be without convictions and deep personal commitments — criticisms usually ascribed to them by those with rigid personalities. The research has shown them to have such confidence in their beliefs that they are not compelled to enshrine them in iron-bound, unyielding systems. Interruptions are expected, though not sought. Leroy could never be a category to such a person — nor could Susan. People with flexibility in their personalities were also found to be less threatened by change and tentative situations. To such a person who was a teacher, both Susan and Leroy would have legitimacy. Susan would be a person who was doing fine technical work in the medium of writing . . . and this talent would be celebrated. Leroy would probably be seen as a person whose talent base for the moment lay elsewhere. The flexible teacher would realize that writing is a skill — and a skill that has high priority in the context of the dominant culture. This teacher would search for a context within which Leroy's talents and skills could emerge. It would be presumed that if Leroy could gain access to expression of his real competence, he might be more comfortable then to explore a medium such as writing, presently so threatening.

With flexibility on the part of the teacher, the concept of multiple talents and skills is considered highly appropriate — and is in fact cherished. To such a teacher, it is normal that people differ. There is also a deep sense of knowing that there are different kinds of thoughts in the meadows of mind. Flexible people know too there are different kinds of genius. Leroy's "street smart" can be seen as a special kind of mindwork — a kind that is highly valued in our culture . . . by those who put a premium on creativity and survival. Susan's apparent "booksmart" dominance is also valued in this culture. However, it is easier to acknowledge. It carries cultural permission and a kind of propriety that nearly everyone can accept. Both are magic . . . and to the flexible person they are gifts. Both Leroy and Susan have a genius — and both are disadvantaged. Only the contexts differ. To the flexible teacher, they both represent incredible energy sources . . . energy to be celebrated. The students as human beings are to be celebrated.

And a good sense of humor? Humor is the commonplace medium of creativity. It is not only the lifeblood of a competent life, but also the training ground for genius. Humor can be viciously aggressive and it can also be unbelievably celebratory. Humor in the classroom is a sculptor of the total learning ecology. This does not mean the teacher becomes a "performer," but rather is a person who is able to create an environment where *the unexpected* is both acknowledged and cherished. Humor nearly always unites ideas and concepts that are disparate. Both Susan and Leroy understand humor.

Care must be taken to avoid the "put down" as a medium of humor. This is the aggressive brand — more typical of Don Rickles, whose style is to "roast." Bill Cosby, on the other hand, is uniquely gifted in seeing the joy and bizarre in everyday life . . . the kind of humor that can nurture life in the classroom.

When people use celebrative humor in environments where learning takes place, they cannot avoid setting an example that nurtures both ways of knowing. What we call rational thought, typified by Susan's skills in writing, establishes the status quo. What we call metaphoric thought often disrupts the status quo — and sends it in new directions. We will talk more about the characteristics of rational and metaphoric thought throughout this book — but for now we remind you that humor has the capacity to nurture both.

In the classroom and throughout life, humor is . . . *surprise.* Jerome Bruner went farther. He called creativity . . . *effective surprise.*

When I know "new"
I feel a sense of joy.

When the world
works in a way
that is outside
my experience

I fill with the awareness
of a total reunion
with the moments
of birth.

Mind meadows are as exciting to harvest as they are to plant. Each person in a lifetime grows and harvests ways of thinking that are best suited for each personally. We as teachers do this — and so do our students — all our lives as we change and grow. If I go into a learner's presence and say, through my overt and tacit actions, that *my* crop this season is the only one with market value, I destroy the possibility of seeing both harvests . . . the other's and mine.

Dreams, thoughts, images, feelings, auras, esp, and a hundred other ways of knowing are all valid and viable. As teachers *and* learners, we can no longer engage in the charade that there is only one way to know. We can create learning settings where many varied ways of learning are recognized . . . and nurtured.

Education is an exploration. Part of it is exploration into the known. This takes place when we as teachers know and encourage students to pick routes into our familiar territory. Other times it is pure exploration into the unknown. Neither we nor the students know what the outcomes will be.

In exploration, the old, formalized rules of a culture must always be tools — never weapons. Susan's facility with these tools must be celebrated — and allowed to cut away the thickets of exclusion that keep Leroy from moving forward. At the same time, we can remember that Leroy's tools of knowing are how survival works . . . and set the course for our expeditions.

Susan deserves an education that does not isolate her to a life encapsulated within society's cliches. She, as a human being with some undeveloped capacities, deserves the opportunity to affirm and develop "street smart." Leroy too deserves more. An educational system that categorically exaggerates the skills of logic isolates Leroy. The effectiveness of "street smart" is heightened by ensuring access to the skills that the dominant culture values. And the skills of logic are enhanced by nurturing "street smart." It is in fact the blending of these modes of knowing that promises to enrich human thought. And a sense of urgency punctuates the enterprise . . . a sense of urgency for the survival of humankind.

3 Meadow Masters

The meadows of mind grow whether tended or not. Nature in its own way provides sun, rain, and urging breezes to the meadows of its own making. So too it is with mind. A child in the womb uses its mind. So too does each of us, regardless of the formal structure of the games of knowledge cherished by our culture. Navajo children know . . . Canadian children know . . . Samoan and African children know. All of us know. Even in deep sleep our minds continue to prowl like gentle predators through the misty pathways of consciousness.

At the same time, all of the minds of humans are strongly affected by the culture in which they grow. Some cultures value some mind meadows more than others do. In the dominant American culture, it is seldom enough for things just to grow — it is further required that the growth be classified and compared to some agreed on standard. *Any meadow won't do.* In education, as in all other human enterprises within our culture, there are tendencies to observe, judge, and assess the nature of growth. Whether this is normal or natural is not the issue here. Instead, the issue is what it means to those who are judged and to those who do the judging in the process of education.

As students of the human mind, psychologists have for decades wandered different routes and found different meadows. In this chapter we will try to see how these varied and diverse routes have tended to affect the ways teaching and learning take place.

The meadow masters — the psychologists who create the vision of human learning — are real. They have structured the philosophical view of what constitutes learning and growth as it exists throughout the United States in our public and most private schools today. In their own ways, the meadow masters provide us with the psychological tools and the rules by which we judge one another as well as ourselves. Educators tend to translate all this into action. Through administrators, consultants, resource people, and teachers, the vision of psychologists becomes learning experiences.

The routes of the masters have been varied. Some are formal and rigorous, while others are more playful and nonintrusive.

What we do here in THE WHOLESCHOOL BOOK is paint broad-brush portraits of the meadow masters. We have selected a few of the most significant who are representative of the major philosophies of psychology affecting teaching and learning today. Our portraits are far from complete. But this introduction to the meadow masters is an attempt to enhance an awareness of what we all know.

A group of five knowledgeable psychologists came to see an elephant. All of them were blind in their own way. One, a Freudian, went immediately to the rear of the elephant and explained its behavior from this chosen view. The behaviorist struck the elephant on the kneecap and was kicked across the courtyard. There she sat planning a positive reinforcement program for young elephants. The cognitive psychologist began to coax the elephant into doing things so that its stage of development could be determined. The humanist felt its ears and tried to convince the elephant that it could fly. The transpersonal psychologist never showed up, and some argued that in reality the transpersonal psychologist was the elephant.

Meadows of Shadow

Though Sigmund Freud can hardly be called a psychologist of education, it is clear that his vision of the human condition persists into the present. Freud, a prolific and temperamental genius, was the most influential person in Western psychology in creating a lasting image of a particular sort about the basic nature of human beings. He saw the human psyche as a pair of warring worlds in which the higher qualities of good and virtue are in constant combat with the qualities of evil and animalism. Humans are both gods and beasts in the Freudian vision, with the beast constantly trying to overwhelm the god.

Freud, powerfully influenced by Charles Darwin and the post-Victorian era, lived his career searching out the subconscious, what others have called the basement of the psyche. He devised models of neurosis, psychosis, repression, and suppression that formed the basis for psychotherapy.

Freud's vision of psychology was dominantly negative. This was undoubtedly because his source of experience was that array of humans we would most often call "mentally ill." Searching through shattered minds is hardly a hopeful starting place to create an image of human mental processes that can guide our vision of education. Yet this is the legacy left to us by Freud. His creation of the id, ego, and superego formed a structure of mindwork that rests with us to this very day.

Though Freud's insights were brilliant, his writings and his theories remained vague and obscure. Nearly two generations of psychologists and psychiatrists made careers out of interpreting and modifying his work. His own tempestuous personality made him demand loyalty of his students and banish them to a kind of exile if they didn't follow his dictates to the letter. He angrily terminated friendships with those who disagreed with him or struck out on their own.

Today Freud's influence is felt mostly by innuendo. There is no doubt that many of the group of psychologists described as behaviorists emerged in order to try to create a "scientific" perspective to counter the highly subjective views of the human condition popularized by Freud's work. In addition, Freud's brand of psychology has lent itself well to the Puritan ethic. His theories described psychological counterparts to "good" and "evil" that fit well with prevailing social philosophies.

Even today, students who are social nonconformists are considered to have problems. Freud's main legacy was to teach us to focus on that which is *wrong* with human beings as opposed to that which is right.

Other psychologists in the therapeutic tradition are far more hopeful. Though their origins were Freudian, Erik Erikson and Richard M. Jones have affected education with visions that are a blending of therapeutic and humanistic traditions. It is for the future to more effectively introduce the positive work of these two scholars to common classroom practice.

Activities

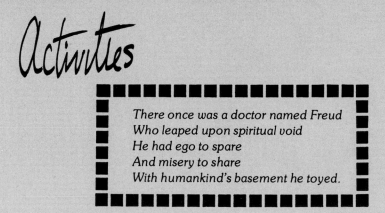

There once was a doctor named Freud
Who leaped upon spiritual void
He had ego to spare
And misery to share
With humankind's basement he toyed.

Students should be seen and not heard . . .
They might say something embarrassing.

Anything embarrassing that students do is due to childhood trauma, related to
parental conflict, manifested in attitude toward the teacher. Therefore, nothing is
really your fault. Interpret problems between you and the students in terms of
your perfection and their "sickness". Assume everyone is filled with repression
and subconscious desires. Explain behaviors in five minutes that you see:
— on the playground
— in class
— in the cafeteria
— in the office
— etc.

Do the previous activity in terms of your own behavior for five minute periods in
the same places.

The next time you feel joyful determine what is wrong with you . . . Once you
know then feel guilty about it.

Meadows of Science

Modern times bring with them in our culture a deep, ingrained respect bordering on reverence for that which can be *measured*. As such, the measureable qualities that each object possesses lend themselves to scientific expression. Those qualities that cannot be measured are shunted off into the arenas of the mystical and generally are not dealt with. Measuring is the primary medium of science. *Behaviorism* is the favorite philosophy of scientifically predisposed psychologists.

Today's *meadow master of behaviorism* is Burrhus Frederick Skinner. Though many of his disciples abound in educational circles, he reigns supreme as the contemporary theorist of this vision. Basically, behaviorism and Skinner's particular vision of it are simple in concept. What is required is an organism that is stimulated. Stimulated by any number of outside actions in such a way that the organism responds.

Here's how it works:

The organism is presented with a stimulus. It catches its attention. The stimulus can be either positive (attractive) or negative (aversive).

In either case, it causes a response. In the example shown, the person responded positively to the 7-Up.

This linkage is a little more complicated, as the person was stimulated by something that cannot be seen. Thus the stimulus is invisible to the observer and must be explained by inference.

All that one can see is the behavior. When the person goes to the refrigerator and gets the ice and 7-Up, the behavior can be explained by saying that the person has been conditioned to go to the refrigerator to fulfill the stimulation.

The appeal of behavioristic explanations for the human condition is simple. They are logical. Though the two examples used above by no means exhaust the possibilities of the analysis of behavior, they do illustrate the simplistic nature of the art. More complex human behaviors, such as falling in love, are explained with more elaborate networks of primary, secondary, and tertiary stimuli with the same series of levels of conditioned responses.

Behaviorism is basically a philosophy of dichotomies. Its vision is analogous to the way digital computers work. It is a philosophy of psychology rich in mechanical metaphors. ON-OFF switches, attraction-repulsion, positive-negative. Furthermore, its techniques are primarily those of mechanical interfaces. Electric shocks, mazes, and mechanical feeders abound in the basic research modes of behaviorism.

The primary application of behaviorism in our culture is with those labeled as deviants of one sort or another. Behaviorism's technique, behavior modification, is most effectively applied to those who are socially, emotionally, physically, or psychologically handicapped. More research has been gathered that shows low levels of effectiveness of behavior-modification techniques with children and adults who are healthy, competent, and nonhandicapped. That doesn't keep advocates of behavior-modification techniques from trying to get them used extensively in our public schools. Most nonhandicapped students seem to recognize behavior modification as being coercive and trivial. Further, it tends to "talk down" to those on whom it is used.

One cannot presume to modify another's behavior without presuming a position of superiority. The *modifier* is essentially the controller. The *modified* is the subject. Thus built into this system is a tacit kind of philosophical chauvinism not at all unlike the prejudices of adultism, sexism, and racism.

Skinner sees all of human learning as a webbed, cross-woven series of conditioned experiences in which stimulus-response linkages explain all of that which is known. Education then becomes the setting for selecting, administering, and evaluating the proper series of conditioning acts. Skinner sees no role for individual exercise of *will*, freedom of choice, or any of the intrinsic qualities relating to the spiritual side of humans. He speaks of creating a social structure that attends to the appropriate kinds of conditioning strategies for all its members. In such a culture, Skinner maintains, the myth of freedom and the absurd notion of intrinsic human dignity would be absent. Absent because they are ideas which are counterproductive to the efficient functioning of society.

Activities

There once was a doctor named Skinner
Who sought a Utopian winner
The thought never took
For no one would cook
M and M entrees for dinner.

If students can exercise no will . . . How come they do so many things I don't want them to?

Only laugh at "good" jokes; your classroom will at all times be silent. Check your supplies for:
— cattleprods
— M and M's
— gold stars
— smiley face stickers

Positive Reinforcement Games

Make a list of compliments you get for one week. Then at the end of the week cross out the ones that:
— were trivial
— were not sincere
— were condescending
— were stupid
— etc.

Repeat the above by listing compliments you *give* for a week.

Meadows of Logic

In terms of contemporary influence, neither Freud nor Skinner dominates the educational scene as much as the twinkling-eyed, soft-spoken Swiss psychologist Jean Piaget. Nearly 50 years ago Piaget began making exhaustive notes about the behavior of his own children as they grew. He noted certain specific stages of logical thought developing in what he thought were sequential stages. Since his interest was primarily in logic and the growth of abstract reasoning, he focused on this aspect of mental processes. He was often heard to say that his interest was in the logical workings of the conscious and that the capricious nature of the unconscious was not his preference.

Piaget devised a host of tasks that demonstrated various levels of logical maturity. By asking children to perform the tasks, he could determine whether or not they were at a particular developmental level. (These levels will be discussed more fully in Chapter 4.)

For example, if a child kept looking for a toy after it was hidden by some kind of barrier, the child would be deemed at a particular level of intellectual maturation. The basis for this conclusion rests on the assumption that the child is beyond "out of sight, out of mind," a view of the world so common in early infancy. In formal terminology, if the child lost interest in the hidden toy, a Piagetian psychologist would say that the child did not yet have object constancy.

Other tasks are related to number, volume, and mass. Each exercise adds a new twist to the child's ability to reason in the abstract. Logical thought, as Piaget sees it, is marked by one's ability to reason without having direct experience with objects and processes. He argues convincingly that children progress through these stages naturally and need not be rushed. Educators in this country are an impatient lot, and many educational strategies have been devised to enhance movement toward abstract, logical thought.

Piaget's premises are easily tested. The levels of development are to a large extent easy to identify. However, his critics are growing in number. Many question whether or not this developmental sequence is a natural part of human growth. Perhaps it is a product of the culture within which we live.

Jerome Bruner, another cognitive psychologist, has done research on West African children, members of the same tribe. The children raised in the African bush were seldom able to achieve any of Piaget's higher levels of development without training. On the other hand, children of the same African tribe who were raised in a highly urban, technological city readily attained the higher developmental levels. This and other evidence has suggested to many that Piaget's work is culturally biased. Some may claim that all this may be academic, however, as our culture is highly technological, and Piaget's developmental stages do seem to apply well to the intellectual, logical maturation of our children.

However, it is clear that developmental approaches are only as complete as the qualities that are chosen to show growth. Piaget and others have chosen the learner's ability to demonstrate abstract, logical modes of thinking as their primary criterion. Many argue that this ignores a more holistic — what we like to call synergic — kind of thinking. The kind of thinking that nurtures creativity. But much more will be said about this later in THE WHOLESCHOOL BOOK.

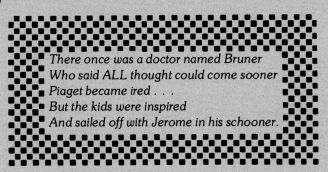

There once was a doctor named Bruner
Who said ALL thought could come sooner
Piaget became ired . . .
But the kids were inspired
And sailed off with Jerome in his schooner.

Logic is the payoff.
Technology couldn't build a better mousetrap.

Basic to cognitive maturity as defined by psychologists is the ability to think about processes, events and relationships that one has not experienced. List the times during a day that you ask the students to think about things they have *not* experienced. Do the same for yourself.

Prove that logic is not logical.

Attempt to think like Mr. Spock on Star Trek.

Prove that intuition is not real (or not logical).

Invent a logical system for:
— a new language
— a new way to count
— a new way to grade
— etc.

Make a list of any ten beliefs . . . then check to see if they are logical.

List all of one's beliefs that are not based on experience.

If you normally teach older students, go to a kindergarten classroom and teach any concept in an intellectually honest fashion. What really is intellectually honest?

Find out what you think is logical that students do not consider to be logical. (For example, the rules you set up to organize the classroom.)

Meadows of Person

Carl Rogers and Abraham Maslow can best be considered as spokespersons for the "whole human." Freud gave us the vision of the role of conscious and subconscious processes at war in humans, whereas Skinner promotes the supremacy of behavioral experience. To Freud, most of learning is genetic and comes from within. To Skinner, genes have little to do with the issue — it is experience and the psychological habits born of that experience that matter. Piaget tends to blend both visions, with an emphasis on the way the genetic and experiential factors blend to structure the development of intellect. Rogers and Maslow saw all of these approaches as limiting and extended the vision of humanness into realms of emotion, feeling, spirituality, and creativity.

The humanistic psychologists have often been called the "third force" psychologists. They are those who celebrated the concept of person beyond the Freudian "first force" vision of good-evil, past Skinner's "second force" behaviorism, and past the narrow, specialized focus of Piaget. Humanistic psychologists are concerned deeply with what is inside the person as well as with what surrounds the person. They celebrate all the facets of humanness at once. Intellectuality, emotionality, and sexuality are equally important. One does not take precedence over any other.

The main distinction of "first force," or Freudian, approaches is that they focused on those who were mentally ill or at least highly troubled. Behaviorism, "second force" psychology, reduces people to objects of scientific analysis.

The humanistic focus encourages "first force" psychologists to experience humans who are well, competent, secure people. To the behaviorists, the humanists urge a realization that behavior is a small slice of the total repertoire of being that represents the whole human.

Whereas Freud saw humans as victims of their egos and behaviorists see humans as recipients of their egos from environmental influence, the humanists see human beings as the creators of their egos. "They built their psychic houses," say humanists of people. "Now they can choose whether to live in them, remodel, or move to another neighborhood." Humanists see each human being as the primary architect of his or her own psychic being.

Maslow worked primarily as a theorist in the philosophy of self-actualization — creating a theory that celebrates not only what a human *is*, but also what a human *could be*. Maslow often said that whereas Freud studied the basement of the human psyche, he (Maslow) studied the attic.

Rogers, a therapist, shocked a whole generation of therapists when he invented an approach which focused on the client rather than on the therapist or on the theory. As quiet as this thrust would appear to be, it was a whole-scale revolution in psychotherapy. To those in education, it represented a philosophy of psychology that put the student as a person at the focal point of the learning process.

The humanistic force in psychology is an emergent force. It is with us now and is being practiced in less than a third of the school settings. It is not organized in the tidiness of behaviorism or the cognitive approaches of Piaget. It is far less accessible to evaluation. It requires at the present time a far broader commitment on the part of teachers than do the earlier "forces." As a result, it can best be represented as a dawning influence on education rather than as a widely practiced philosophy of psychology and educational psychology.

Activities

There was a young doctor named Maslow
Who explored the way people could grow
He made a long list
Of things that were missed
By those who thought humans so-so.

It's hard to be actualized when you're hungry.

Look at any set of lesson plans that you write and make a list of ten things that you *cannot* do if you carry out those plans.

Encourage the students to create the same kind of list after looking at your lesson plans.

Choose any two things from the students' list and do them. In turn have them choose from your list and do the same.

Publish your lesson plans and distribute them to the students. Have them grade your plans and return them.

Work for getting "mental health" days as legitimate leave days in your school system.

Share peak experiences with the students.

Distinguish between the following:
— peek experience
— pique experience
— peak experience

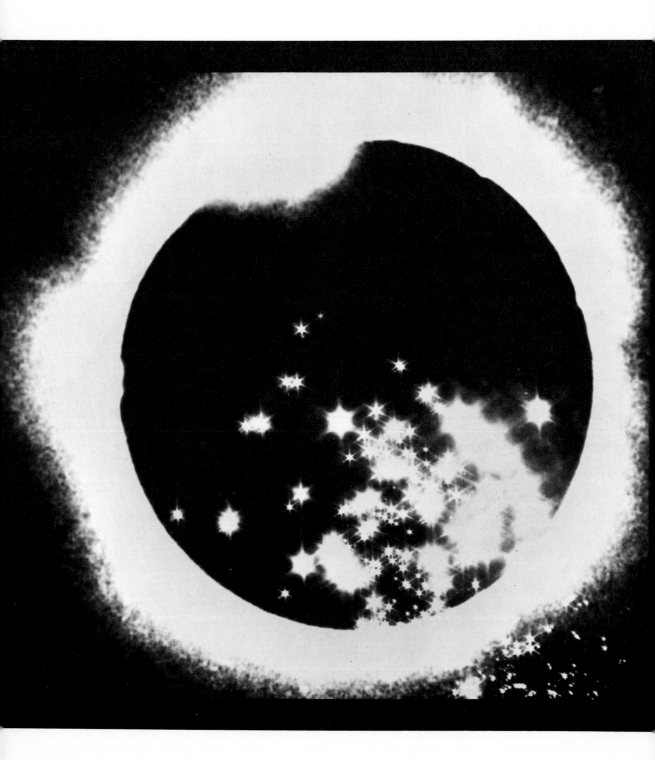

Meadows of Cosmos

The "fourth force" in psychology is even less common than the humanistic, "third force." The "fourth force" is a way of viewing the human condition that is filled with spirituality, mysticism, and psychic qualities that transcend all that have preceded it. It is rightfully labeled *transpersonal psychology*.

Currently there is no specific person who can be identified as its leader. Always appearing to be on the fringe of what could be considered serious and proper, transpersonal psychology has had a hazardous course throughout its history. Only recently have highly respected psychologists, neurophysiologists, and a host of other scientists begun to consider this a legitimate field.

In education some of the folk wisdom common to the teaching experience is found in the often-heard remark, "The kids are really hyper . . . there's bound to be a change in the weather!" Such statements are frequently attributed to rather hazy and difficult-to-pin-down feelings and intuitions. "Vibes," a more recently coined word, is linked to the unstated, nonverbal sensations people often get in situations charged with emotions. Most often, these sensations are dismissed as irrational and nonlogical. Yet through rather intriguing ways of photographing ordinarily nonvisible energy, it can easily be demonstrated that energy fields around the human body are common. Many people claim to be able to see such "auras."

Dreams, which to many schools of psychology are little more than personal laboratories of neurosis, are being shown to be far more. Dreams can apparently be sent over long distances. And one person's dreams often impinge on another's. Dreams can be arenas for heightening self-esteem and self-concept. They can also be the wellsprings for rather remarkable creative involvement.

41

Though evidence is still being gathered, it is clear that there is far more to the transpersonal arguments than it has been popular to acknowledge. Interest in this field is growing among researchers, doctors, surgeons, and educators. The strength and weakness of transpersonal views lie in the same point. The transpersonal psychologist assumes that the person is part of and accessible to larger systems of knowing, with perhaps the entire cosmos a part of knowing. Critics seize this assumption as being unfounded and irrational. Yet these same critics stand on a data base that started out the same way. Isaac Newton, Copernicus, and Galileo were courageous as they faced what was then the unknown.

Classical science has labeled five senses for humans — seeing, hearing, tasting, touching, and smelling. Of these, as we have said, seeing and hearing usually dominate the educational experience. More recently, touching has again been recognized to be important for almost any age learner — "hands on," direct manipulation of objects and learning materials has become a vital part of instruction.

Research is beginning to indicate that multisensory involvement enriches the experience and makes it far more lasting. Transpersonal psychologists are thus convinced that if having only the five classical senses "turned on" improves learning, look what will happen when we allow access to *all* the human abilities! Some of these psychologists suggest that perhaps 15 or 20 other senses are present at birth and have been allowed to atrophy away. There are those who argue that some humans can sense geomagnetic forces, electrical induction, barometric changes, nonvisible areas of the electromagnetic spectrum, and perhaps even a kind of human magnetism produced by life energy. Some children become hyperactive when flourescent bulbs do not contain the total spectrum. Research has shown that some people who are placed in sensory-deprivation chambers can sense other people's presence even when the intruders are dozens of feet away.

When transpersonal psychologists speak of education in the future, they visualize learning becoming multisensory in a way we can only speculate about now. Far from becoming passive human robots into which knowing will be directed, humans will probably become awesomely more vital. By turning on one's full spectrum of senses, even what appear to be trivial and commonplace experiences will become fuller and richer than we could suspect. It is apparent that the people of genius in history and in the present have a greater flexibility and facility with information than those lesser gifted. For too long the presumption has been that these people were simply more intelligent — more logical. Now transpersonal psychologists are inviting us to ask the question, "Is there *more* to intelligence than tradition has shown us?" There seems to be little doubt there is.

Activities

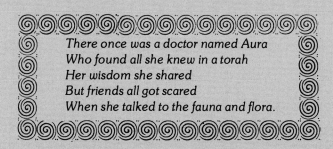

There once was a doctor named Aura
Who found all she knew in a torah
Her wisdom she shared
But friends all got scared
When she talked to the fauna and flora.

Just because I'm enlightened doesn't mean I'm competent.

Determine the commonness of transpersonal experiences in your class.

Use dreams as the basis for the study of political science.

Determine which of your students have more than five senses.

Explore Deja Vu and see if it can be done intentionally.

Hypnotize your principle . . . and see what principal is served.

SHADOW SCIENCE LOGIC PERSON COSMOS

Back and Forth

Inside the classroom is a gaggle of more or less captive human beings. Some are adult, some are not. All are a blend of security, fear, weakness, strength, compassion, and capacity. For the teacher, this blend is critical. The teacher stays.

Year after year, 181 days pass . . . the teacher stays, the students move on.

Thus there are two sides to the coin of psychology. One side relates to the teacher, who stays. And the other relates to the students, who pass through. Let's look at the way this works.

Many times in the preceding pages, the words "psychology" and "philosophy" have been wedded. Psychology is a philosophy. The only way psychological philosophies differ is in how they view the human in the context of their framework. Freudian philosophy sees humans basically as a battleground between good and evil. Thus the psychology reflects this vision.

Behaviorists look at small slices of the total human, packaged in the way the person behaves. The philosophy is linked to objectivity and analytic science. Thus the psychology is basically mechanical and clinical.

Cognitive psychology is a philosophy of intelligence. Its methods stand somewhere between the behaviorists and the humanists and blend so well with both that cognitive psychology never rose to the status of a "force." To practice its philosophy, one looks for the development of logic and reason as the primary payoff.

The philosophy of humanism is a response toward humans that presumes that they are "good," whereas Freudian approaches were full of the suspicion that they are evil. In addition, humanistic philosophy took severe issue with the "human as an object" vision of the behaviorists. The humanists moved past Freud's notion that most human problems are linked to a basic animalistic tendency and the opposite view, held by the behaviorists, that all is the result of one's experience in the environment.

44

The transpersonal psychologists have extended the view of the humanistic philosophy into the natural systems of the cosmos. They are ready and eager to defend the idea that all things in the universe are connected. Though there is no attempt to link human existence with any cause-and-effect philosophy, the transpersonal psychologists are unwilling to rule out the interaction of forces, energies, and senses that we currently know little about.

Now to get back to how this philosophical-psychological vision affects teachers and students. The teacher is the dominant controlling element of the kind of human ecology that emerges in the classroom. Thus teachers tend to control their *own* vision of the psychological environment and as a result control the primary quality of the environment the students will experience.

All of the philosophical-psychological postures — Freudian, behaviorist, cognitive, humanist, and transpersonal — are valid. But they are valid within certain limits. Each of these philosophical-psychological postures is focused on somewhat different areas of the human spectrum. In addition, there is a difference in how comprehensive each vision is.

For example, humanistic psychology is far broader in its approach to the human condition than either the behavioristic or cognitive approaches. Yet transpersonal psychology is more comprehensive than all.

What this means to the teacher is that "you get what you pay for." When people choose one philosophical-psychological approach over another, they get what is inherent within that approach. Behaviorism provides far more certainty and specificity than humanistic and transpersonal approaches. Humanistic and transpersonal psychologies are far richer than behaviorism by including a greater array of human qualities seen as vital to the process of learning. Humanistic and transpersonal perspectives are *inclusive* rather than *exclusive* systems. Both include those versions of psychological vision termed behaviorial and cognitive. However, the opposite is not true; behavioral and some cognitive approaches tend to deny that which cannot be measured and validated.

Though let us take care. On these pages we do not intend that *any* psychology be wholly excluded in favor of others. Our real intent is to communicate that there are many ways to view human beings and how they learn. Life seen solely from within *any* meadow has its rewards and its penalties. There are times when it is a joy to be specific, other times when it is a joy to revel in ambiguity.

In the final consideration, there is the realization that in each of our experiences we have the right to choose. If our experience does not include more than one option, this is no choice at all.

As a teacher, I owe it to myself first and to the students second to get experience, choosing from the richest possible array of options. No philosophical-psychological posture is right — at least not all the time! None is wrong. They are different and do different things. Each creates and describes different environments within which to live and learn. All of us exist within those environments . . . teachers, students, parents, administrators . . . all of us.

4

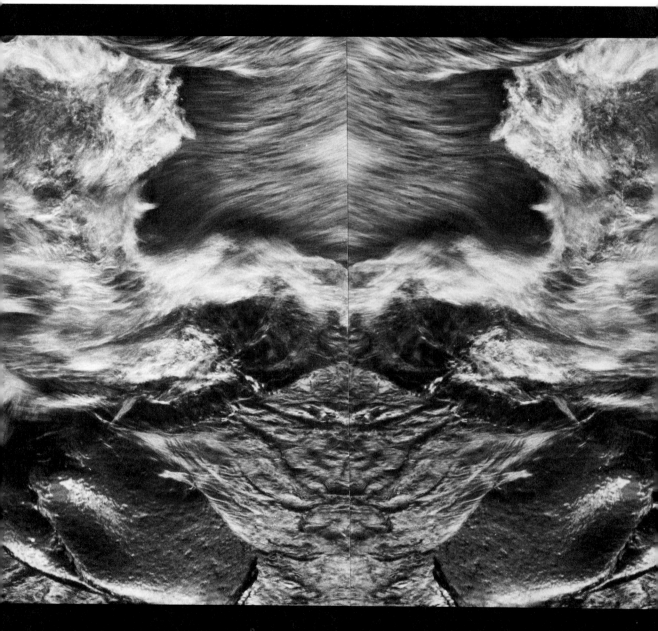

A Mighty River Flows

We have been making casual reference to brain functions and physiology. It is time to be a bit more specific. Let us pretend for a moment that each of us has within our heads not just *one* meadow — but two. Two distinctly different meadows. Since they are both meadows, certainly they have some qualities in common. But still there are distinct differences about them. To show you how separate they are, visualize a wide and swiftly flowing river between them. That's it — a river between them, flowing from one hemisphere to the other.

The awesome feature of this river is that it flows both ways at once. Substance from one meadow can instantly flow into the other. However, as soon as it arrives, it is transformed into the ecology of that new meadow. Now if you are not quite ready for a river that flows both ways at once, just read on. We promise to come back to this idea later.

Recent neurophysiological research indicates that each of us has within us two distinctly different halves, or hemispheres, of the brain. That is — though obviously each has much in common with the other, being part of the same general substance and structure — each hemisphere houses functions which are quite different from those of the other.

The left hemisphere, in most of us in our society, houses primarily those functions identified as being linear, logical, and sequential. This is the home of rationality; haven of analytical processes; and reservoir of abstract, logical thought. This is the "orderly," "tidy," and in some ways "conventional" half of our brain. It has the ability to take a number of stimuli and focus in on those that are most "logically" appropriate. In part because it does so well with order and sequence, it is the half of the brain that typically houses the mechanisms for such skills as speaking, reading, and writing — and even that other "R," arithmetic. Simply stated, understanding grammar and its uses is a primary function of the left cerebral hemisphere. Problem solving, through careful deduction or induction, is in large part a function of the left cerebral hemisphere; in these cases, it is those aspects of the problem solving that move in a sequential, orderly, logical fashion, frequently making competent use of analytical processes. The left cerebral hemisphere actually seems to function, then, in a manner described by Piaget in his levels of intellectual maturity. (Remember Chapter 3, "Meadow Masters"?) The Piagetian hierarchy of development — in the four stages from sensorimotor through formal operations — seems to be a fairly accurate portrait of left cerebral hemispheric development in our society.

But recent neurophysiological findings support the notion that the other hemisphere in most of us does not, in fact, operate in the fashion of the left cerebral hemisphere. The right cerebral hemisphere is now being shown to house a number of qualities that humans have recognized in themselves for generations . . . but found difficult to describe. One likely reason for the difficulty in describing these qualities is that among other things, the right cerebral hemisphere does not usually carry out the language functions that the left cerebral hemisphere does. That is, in most of us, the right cerebral hemisphere does not house the mental networks that perform the major tasks of reading, writing, and computation.

Instead, the right cerebral hemisphere appears to dominate with visualization skills. Abilities such as "hearing" music, as in "playing by ear," are housed in the right cerebral hemisphere — as opposed to the skill of *reading* music, a linear function that appears to be housed in the left cerebral hemisphere.

The right hemisphere has the ability to take numbers of data simultaneously and combine them in unpredictable ways. It can thus deal with data (ideas, concepts, things, etc.) analogically. It can deal rapidly, simultaneously, and capriciously in metaphor. That is, ideas, concepts, and things can take on new meanings, be represented in new ways . . . but not as if by any predetermined or identifiable logic. With these abilities, the right hemisphere has tremendous *inventive* capacities. The right hemisphere sees things in pictures, senses them fully, and frequently manages to slip past the censoring voice of the rational left hemisphere to make its "knowings" known. But let us not forget that without verbal ability, the right hemisphere could not describe the resulting analogic arrangements and complete the magic of discovery.

How can humans effectively explain skills like these? We frequently have turned to words like "intuition." We say things like, "I can't explain it . . . it just popped into my head." Now we're finding that these intuitive leaps, inexplicable feelings of insight, creative but unpredictable solutions to problems, need not be apologized for — but rather are the legitimate functions of one half of each of our brains!

FORMAL OPERATIONS (12 years on) Just as concrete operations are characterized by children's being able to limit variables in thought to abstractions, this stage is characterized by their being able to act on two or more abstractions simultaneously. This means that the child thinks logically about one event (such as balancing two people on a teeter-totter) and comes to resolution about it — and simultaneously considers the effects of another logical abstraction on the process. This would be like first resolving that two children could balance on the teeter-totter and then adding the third child in a special place to maintain the balance. It is a stage of sophisticated logic.

CONCRETE OPERATIONAL (5-12 years) Now children are well on the way to becoming abstract logical thinkers. They can speculate about certain events in the physical environment in such a way that they do not need to experience them through the senses to determine the results. In other words, they substitute mental activity for actual sensory experience. At this time children begin to learn to classify elements of the world. That is, they sort objects into classes that separate them from other classes. Children in this stage have formed certain "laws" of logic. If something happens in opposition to the logic, they presume the event is at fault and *not* the logic.

PRE-OPERATIONAL (2-5 years) This stage is marked by the children's ability to operate on abstractions. That is, they cease being wholly dependent upon what is happening immediately in their environment. They imitate behaviors that happened a long time before, and they visibly begin to demonstrate that they think about things before they do them. In this stage children begin to use language. They use words in sentences during this stage. All in all the child exhibits an ability to begin thinking in abstractions or, as it is called by Piaget, representational thinking. Thought is generally egocentric even though it is abstract; the child's *own* viewpoint seems to dominate and he or she cannot think from another's viewpoint.

SENSORIMOTOR (birth-2 years) The stage at which action takes place with little or no understanding. Early in this stage it is presumed that the child believes that things exist only if they are touched, seen, or heard. If an object is shown to a child and then screened off with a barrier, the child behaves as though the object is gone. When this stage is almost over, children will behave as though they know the object still exists and is only hidden by the barrier. In other words, the child's knowledge is linked specifically to reality of perception. They do not yet do abstract thinking.

50

the stages of Piaget are developmental. As such they are judged by the culture to which they apply. The Metaphoric Modes * are independent of Culture...

* See p.185 for a fuller description.

Piaget's developmental sequence —

As each level is attained the earlier levels tend to be pushed farther into the background of consciousness..

The Metaphoric Modes work this way....

SYMBOLIC ABSTRACT · SYMBOLIC VISUAL · SYNERGIC COMPARATIVE · INTEGRATIVE · INVENTIVE

The Symbolic Abstract is primarily Compatible with the Formal operations level

The Symbolic Visual operates at all stages of development

The Synergic Comparative mode operates at all levels of development

The Integrative mode Operates at all levels of development.

The Inventive Mode Operates at all levels and also tends to include all the others simultaneously.

The real issue is that all these modes work to assist human learning at all times. We have just created a model of schooling that legitimizes only one. It is time to serve the whole human!

You may fairly ask at this point, "Okay, I've got the two meadows — now let's get back to this river between them . . . *a river that flows both ways at once!*"

It seems that in most human beings, somewhere between the ages of three years and five years a fibrous, stubborn sort of separation develops between the two hemispheres of the brain. It is a complex thing, but the major part of this actual physical division between the hemispheres is called the *corpus collosum.* Not that the technical name matters so much, but the concept and its apparent functions do. The corpus collosum serves effectively to monitor the communication between the hemispheres of the brain. Another effect is to allow a set of dominant processes to become isolated and housed uniquely in one hemisphere or the other. Now it certainly appears that communication is shared from hemisphere to hemisphere — across the mighty river of the corpus collosum, so to speak — but not enough in most people to muddy the meadows and make them similar. The dominant functions of each hemisphere remain in most of us quite different, unique, and distinct from the other.

There is no physiological reason to doubt this two-way flow. Yet in terms of conventional logic, the metaphor of the river flowing two ways at once doesn't make sense. The perplexity of this idea, like the Sufi stories we use so often in these pages, contains the key to some level of understanding.

It is undoubtedly a social issue that creates the favor we show to logic in mental action. We live in a culture that cherishes making sense. Our culture cherishes logic, linearity, and rationality. So much so that ideas like a two-way river don't "make sense." But to the right hemisphere, to the metaphoric mind, two-way rivers *make* sense. Even Sufi stores make sense. The mind can operate at dozens of levels. One of these levels is logic. More complex levels are metaphor and intuition. Other levels are typically only ghosts on our consciousness.

We are moving to awarenesses of far more complex uses and functions of mind than we have in the past. The simple concept that the two cerebral hemispheres differ in function is quite threatening to some people. Imagine their consternation when listening to those who discuss the paleo cortex, the limbic system, and those more basal portions of the brain and nervous system!

This vision of the brain and of knowing and learning extends the concept of mind. It extends mind into qualities of function seldom discussed in books about psychology and education. If this is so far out, what is it doing in an educational-methods book?

Simple. You have chosen a profession of mind. Teaching and learning is an art, a science, and a spiritual enterprise. We simply hope to extend the limits of perception so that the meadows of mind will be celebrated . . . those meadows that add and subtract as well as those meadows that joyfully invent and transform. *We also want to celebrate rivers that flow both ways at once!*

Materials needed: crayons, marking pens, wet leaves, anything which can be used for creating art on paper.

Assignment: In the space on this page, create a visual image that symbolizes for you the concept of teaching the *whole mind* of learners.

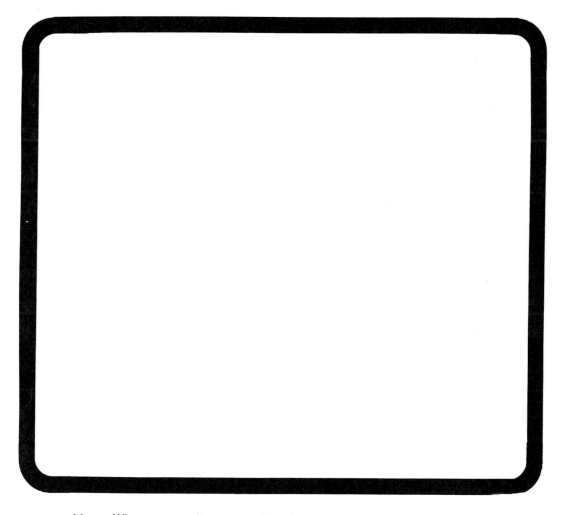

More: Whenever you're engaged in the process of teaching, remember the image. (You will!)

Nasrudin was hearing his first case as judge. The prosecuting attorney brought forth a host of witnesses, offered an extensive assortment of exhibits, and ended with a convincing appeal regarding the defendant's guilt. So impressed was Nasrudin that he jumped up and shouted, "You're right!" as the prosecutor finished his presentation. The defense attorney immediately objected and requested that Nasrudin hear the case for the defense. Many witnesses, exhibits, and summations later, Nasrudin, this time totally impressed with the defense attorney's argument, bolted from his chair and shouted, "You're right!" A juror then protested, "But Your Honor, they can't both be right!" Nasrudin turned to the juror and said, "You're right!"

— An old Sufi story

5

Meadow Paths

Dichotomites to the Rescue?

The meadow masters—those philosophers who created psychology—have each in turn played the role of defense attorney, prosecutor, judge, and juror. To understand the human mind, each investigator has broken it into pieces which are more easily explained. So we have conscious/unconscious, stimulus/response, safety/growth, sick/healthy, cognitive/affective, concepts/processes, intuition/rationality, etc. Each of these pairings serves as a dichotomy and supposedly provides a clearer, analytic view of how human beings function. And if we were to judge each meadow master, we could shout as did Nasrudin, "You're right—but incomplete!"

Only recently has it become popular to question dichotomies. Their presence has become an integral part of the strategies of Western thought. In psychology Freud gave us conscious/unconscious, the behaviorists followed with stimulus/response, the cognitive psychologists created assimilation/accommodation, the humanistic psychologists worried about safety and growth motivation, and now the transpersonal psychologists talk of consciousness and altered states of consciousness.

The Limitations of Context

Contexts are both *contents* and *containers*. The structure of a container is real, and it serves to limit its contents. A bottle filled with wine cannot be a bottle filled with air at the same time. It *can* be a bottle of air if we pour out the wine.

There is, of course, a time and a place for the judgments that we make of the dichotomies we create for the analyses we engage in. That is, "When you're right, you're right!" . . . but only when. It would be dysfunctional, for instance, to insist on the analytical fact that $2 + 2 = 4$ while shopping at a 2-for-1 sale.

Often, however, operational strategies in education are based on analytic judgments which assume that only half of a dichotomy is legitimate. As educators, we often place ourselves only in the role of jurors, and we insist that if the prosecution is right, the defense is wrong. It is at those moments that we should explore *dualism*. Thinking dualistically engages both parts of a dichotomy at once.

A dichotomist turned farmer went to purchase a cow so that he might have milk for his family. He asked the price of a fine-looking Holstein and was told it would cost $400. Not knowing much about cows, he asked where the milk came from. He was shown the udder and noticing that it was not on the front half of the cow, he offered $200 for the rear half.

quiz on the nature of the learner for educators

Directions: Choose the correct response to each item. **Circle only one for each item.**

1. Learners assimilate information using (a) conscious, (b) unconscious processes.
2. The learner's task in a behavioristic system is to produce a (a) stimulus, (b) response.
3. The learner is a creature of (a) safety, (b) growth.
4. The learner is (a) patient, (b) client.
5. The learner needs (a) intellectual skills, (b) love.
6. The learner should (a) know, (b) do.
7. The learner should be (a) artistic, (b) logical.
8. Learners should use their (a) heads, (b) bodies.

"You're RIGHT!" . . . BUT INCOMPLETE no matter how you answer. (We know because we're right!")

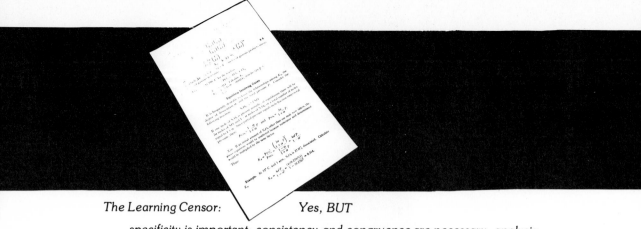

The Learning Censor: *Yes, BUT*

. . . specificity is important; consistency and congruence are necessary; analysis is useful; cognition and precepts lead to order; reflection is indispensable; assimilation is a key faction in evaluation; logic is reality; caution, diligence, tradition, hard work, norms, and not biting off more than you can chew will lead to useful, logical products that can be taught to others.

The Learning Censor is the social conscience of the teacher (student, principal, board member, parent). It is the haunting voice which cries out for accountability. It longs for justification. It seeks reward through producing those disadvantaged subcultures in the neighborhoods of humankind called the "work ethnics." They are disadvantaged—not economically or in terms of social status—but in terms of their own human development and maturation. They are often called well adjusted.

Because the Learning Censor is such an ingrained part of our culture, it is a necessary part of any teacher's personality. Since the censor's skills are easily developed and relatively easily implemented, it is the censor who becomes the overriding influence on many educators and on those educated. If Learning Censors were to do their work as quickly and as simply as the role suggests, education would cease at the end of the first month of each school year.

The Learning Censor's View of Learning

The Learning Censor is a metaphor for a style of learning with the following assumptions:

1. Learning is *work*.
2. Learning is overcoming a *deficiency* (of knowledge).
3. Learning requires understanding of *causes*.
4. Learning is the *analysis* of structured experience in a universe that is ordered.
5. The relevance of what is learned is to be judged by how well it fits with *public or formal knowledge*.

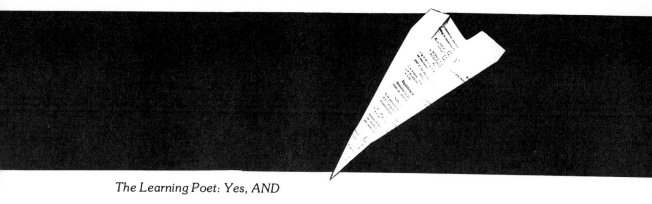

The Learning Poet: Yes, AND

. . . what else? Don't forget ambiguity, inconsistency, incongruity, intuition, perception and percepts, spontaneity, transformation, analogical processes and reality transcendence, disclosure, newness, play, evolution, individuation, and private enhancement.

The Learning Poet, of course, is not concerned with systems of accountability that limit experience in learning. This is not because Learning Poets don't care. It is because they know that the truly important learnings can never be evaluated to the Learning Censor's satisfaction.

The Learning Poet exaggerates, extends, and pushes old ideas to their outer limits. Learning Poets operate in and document those acts of "craziness" which transform the commonplace into new contexts. The censors are frustrated because all they seek is fodder for the cannon of accountability.

The Learning Poet's View of Learning

The Learning Poet is a metaphor for a style of learning with the following assumptions:
1. Learning is *play*.
2. Learning is extending and celebrating *capabilities*.
3. Learning requires becoming an *effect*.
4. Learning is the personal meanings which surface as one *experiences* the universe.
5. The relevance of what is learned is to be judged by its contribution to the learner's personal *informal knowledge*.

The following is an example of how the Learning Censor works:

Lesson Plan

TOPIC: Mathematics
GOAL: To Build Skills of Measurement
OBJECTIVE: The Students will express on paper
the standards of measurement.
MATERIALS: Ruler, String

ACTIVITIES:
   1) Ask the students to use the materials
     to find the width and length of
       a) their workbook
       b) their desk
       c) the room
   2) Discuss the needs for standards of
     measurement.
   3) Introduce the concept of the standard
     platinum bar kept in Washington D.C.
EVALUATION: On a sheet of paper the students
will tell where the standard for length
is kept and why it is needed.

LESSON PLANNED (WRITTEN BY THE LEARNING POET!)

ASSIGNMENT: FIND OUT HOW FAR IT IS TO THE STUDENT STORE. (DON'T USE COP-OUT TOOLS!)

ACTIVITIES: (WRITTEN AFTER STUDENTS DID THE ASSIGNMENT.)

1. BILL — The student store is 123 sidewalk cracks away.
   SUE — The student store is (78 + 93)/2 eyeblinks away.
   TERRI — The student store is 3 medium (2 long) conversations away.
   KENNY — The student store is 3/5 bag of Cornnuts away.
   JILL — The student store is 728 size 6½ shoes away.

2. STUDENTS THEN FOUND OUT HOW MANY SIDEWALK CRACKS = HOW MANY EYEBLINKS = HOW MANY CONVERSATIONS = HOW MANY CORNNUTS = HOW MANY SIZE 6½ SHOES = ...

3. STUDENTS WERE ASKED TO INVENT A WAY TO EFFECTIVELY COMMUNICATE TO THE LEARNING CENSOR THE DISTANCE TO THE STUDENT STORE.

4. STUDENTS INVENTED A STANDARD MEASURE AND AN EASILY AVAILABLE OR PORTABLE REPLICA OF THE STANDARD. (THEY CHOSE THE SMALLEST SHOE SIZE IN THE CLASS AND MARKED THAT SIZE ON THE EDGE OF THE SOLE OF EACH CLASS MEMBER'S SHOE. WE ALSO DISCUSSED THE APPLICABILITY OF THIS STANDARD OF MEASURE TO ABORIGINAL TRIBES. THE CLASS DECIDED THAT FOR THESE TRIBE MEMBERS THE MEASURE DID NOT MATTER ANYWAY. THOUGH THEY MIGHT NOT WEAR SHOES, THEY PROBABLY ALSO WOULD NOT HAVE OCCASION TO WANT TO TALK TO THE LEARNING CENSOR.)

The following analysis completes the record for the Learning Poet's Lesson Planned above:

TOPIC: MATHEMATICS, ARITHMETIC, NUTRITION, P.E., ANATOMY, ARCHITECTURE, SOCIAL STUDIES

GOAL: INDIVIDUATION AND PRIVATE ENHANCEMENT OF PUBLIC KNOWLEDGE

OBJECTIVE: SEE ACTIVITIES

EVALUATION: YOU'RE KIDDING! BUT IF YOU'RE NOT, EVERY CRITERION FOR STANDARD UNITS OF MEASURE APPLIES. ALL THAT DIFFERS ARE THE UNITS.

This apparent dichotomy between the Learning Censor and the Learning Poet is really a duality. The poet and censor are not mutual enemies. Instead, they act like light and shadow. They are interdependent in ways that celebrate both.

Effective classroom teachers who nurture independence, decision making, and creativity in their students seem to have established the Learning Censor and the Learning Poet in a pattern of mutual respect. For these teachers, their Learning Poet provides lots of data for the censor. And the Learning Censor protects the poet by pacifying the conscience of accountability. These teachers seem to have made pluralistic partners instead of dichotomous adversaries out of their censors and poets.

Celebrating *both* the Learning Poet and the Learning Censor is something it is up to teachers to do . . . because few instructional materials do so.

Teacher:	Let's turn to the logic lesson in your workbook. Turn to page 87.
Teacher:	Who would like to read number 1? Michelle?
Michelle:	Which of the following does not belong? Doctor, Lawyer, Robber, Minister.
Teacher:	Aaron! Which do you think?
Aaron:	Minister.
Teacher:	Why?
Aaron:	All the others are rip-off artists.
Teacher:	You're right!
Linda:	I don't agree. A robber provides job security for policemen!
Teacher:	You're right!
Class:	But teacher, *everybody can't be right!*
Teacher:	O.K.! I'd like you to break into four groups. Each group will be responsible for proving a different one of the choices is correct . . . and for deciding which answer the author expected.
Teacher:	(whispers to self) Sufi so good!

64

Neither the Learning Censor nor the Learning Poet exists except as a metaphor for how the human mind functions. Both are entities we create to help us understand and make more effective use of our total human functioning. Whatever image you choose can be useful to describe the functions of mind.

We find it rather easy to relate to a bespectacled, tidy, conservatively dressed middle manager of some official agency, running round in our heads doing evaluation and cost-benefit analyses of the way we think. Our Learning Censor is always seeking the "proper," most efficient way of presenting ideas. For censors, an adequate reward would be that all the decimal places were in the right location, the figures added up, and that they were offered a gold watch on retirement. Often we are a bit embarrassed by the censor's narrow-mindedness and plodding style. We're also often a bit frustrated by the censor's overemphasis on the tidiness of language and logic. This overemphasis gets a bit limiting. However, there is much sympathy and support for the censor, particularly when a person wants to find something exactly where it was left. With the censor, things are always where you want them when you need them.

Our Learning Poet, on the other hand, is an irreverent rascal. It always pokes fun at the censor. With broad strokes of pen, brush, tongue or whatever is available . . . the poet is always satirizing or exaggerating the limited view of the universe that analysis brings us. We find ourselves laughing with and applauding the muse while at the same time being a bit awestruck and frightened of its deviant wisdom. *

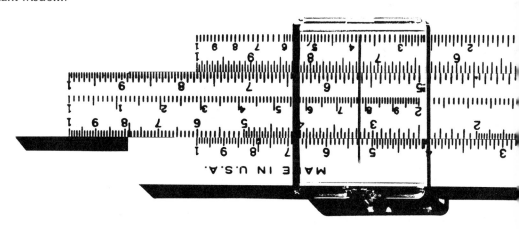

* We have borrowed descriptions of the Learning Censor and the Learning Poet from Richard M. Jones, based on his portraits of the dream censor and dream poet. The whole concept of learning censor and poet is taken directly from Richard's brilliant assessment of how dreams can be viewed. More than likely we are attempting to make literal for education what Richard described in the context of dream exploration but, knowing Richard, likely intended as a metaphor for living.

"The Best Surprise is No Surprise" . . . *Sometimes.*

As teachers, learners, and human beings (not necessarily mutually exclusive categories), we have desire of some mechanism to simplify our complex universe, if only to maintain our sanity. The Learning Censor serves this function well, filtering the infinite variety of data which bombard us each moment into understandable patterns. The Learning Censor focuses on data which justify what we already know. It helps us formulate and predict. Further, the Learning Censor also helps us to establish and make use of organized information and experience so as to be understood by those with whom we come in contact. This helps to avoid confusion and keeps us from upsetting one another.

The Learning Censor thus helps us to recognize and construct a world that is familiar, predictable, and efficient. It gives us the security of entering a situation and being able to say, "I've done this before, and I feel that I know how to function appropriately." The Learning Censor helps us to find and build "old places" even in new experience. These are places where the parameters are known, the data collectible, and the outcomes predictable. In other words, the censor helps us build things that are safe and have few surprises.

The Learning Censor built the Holiday Inn. In schools it sets up routines to take roll, collect milk money, salute the flag, correct workbooks, and teach all the things that the culture thinks are safe enough to teach without controversy. Also, the Learning Censor takes weekends and holidays off.

But Isn't It Surprising How . . .

There is another human characteristic, however, which seeks newness, the unexpected, the excitement of ambiguity. This aspect of humanness is searching to extend itself beyond the realm of justification and expectation. It seeks to invent communication channels which transcend the limitations of shared language. In fact, it appears to extend beyond the very structures of language. It operates in the realm of limitless data and it thrives on surprise. This is the realm of the Learning Poet. The Poet continually seeks "new places," and if allowed, it often builds them on "old places."

A Polar Bare

It is important to be reminded that the Learning Poet and the Learning Censor are dualistic rather than dichotomous. That is, *they are not inherently polar.* Polarity is an exaggeration of the distance between, and the compulsion to separate, related qualities. Polarity is a prejudicial posture. It has produced racism, adultism, sexism, and each of the other forms of human prejudice that exist today. By actively supporting only one half of a dichotomy and/or actively repressing its counterpart, we ensure a condition whereby the special characteristics of both parts can never be harmoniously integrated or each appropriately engaged.

Chapter 1 of THE WHOLESCHOOL BOOK, "Mind Meadows," introduced us to just such a dichotomy turned polar. The avenue of the three "L's" of logic, linearity, and language are highly valued in Western culture and assumed to lead to the freeway of the three "R's" of reading, 'riting, and arithmetic, which are even more highly valued. When this valuing becomes excessive, as it appears to be in many classrooms, there is a price to pay.

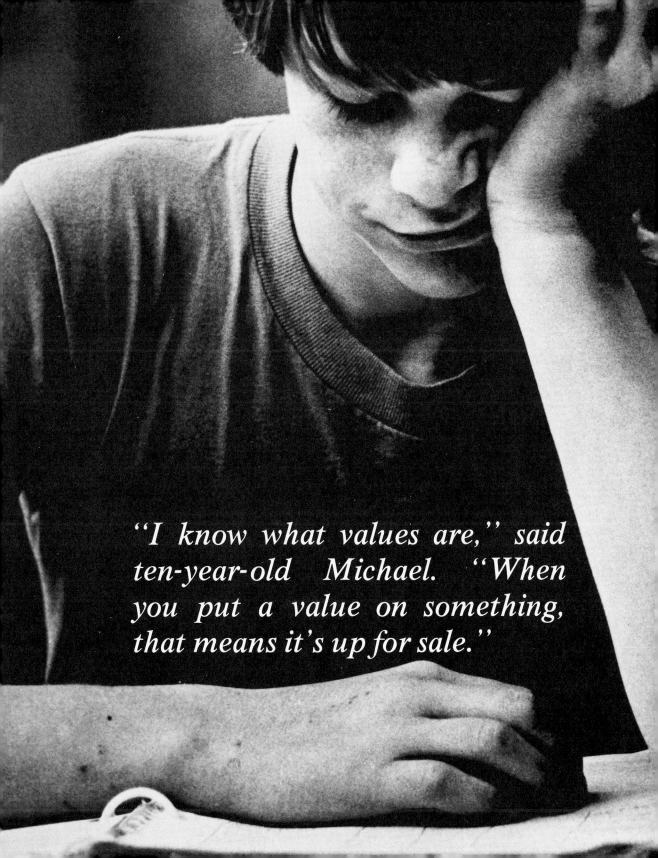

"I know what values are," said ten-year-old Michael. "When you put a value on something, that means it's up for sale."

Nasrudin was a boatman and provided a shuttle service across a large lake for the people of the region. One day a scholar had need of Nasrudin's service, and soon they were far out on the lake, with Nasrudin happily singing his boatman's song. The scholar attempted to engage the boatman in conversation and asked Nasrudin about some well-known literary work. "I ain't never heard of it" was the reply. The scholar admonished, "My good man, have you never studied grammar?" "No, I ain't," came the reply. "Why, then, you've wasted half your life." As Nasrudin continued his singing, a storm came up and the small boat began to fill, tossing precariously on the now wave-torn surface of the lake. Nasrudin turned to the scholar and queried, "Sir, have you ever learned to swim?" "No," replied the scholar. "Then I'm afraid that all of your life has been wasted, since our craft is about to sink."

—An old Sufi story

The price that is paid for overvaluing rationality is the price of polarizing the mind. At first there is the simple reverence (for rationality) which accompanies any new religion. This is followed rapidly, however, by repression of the counterforces, in this case the domain of the Learning Poet, the metaphoric mind.

It's Time for a Seize Your

The Learning Censor and Learning Poet are closely connected to what we call the rational and the metaphoric minds. The prejudice which produces adults with little direct access to their metaphoric processes correlates highly with the forces which allow us greater use of our Learning Censor than our Learning Poet. It would be a simple task to play the role of apologist for the Learning Poet here and to support a school system which highly values the muse. There are many educators who, in responding to the suppression of the Learning Poet, have reacted by turning the tables. Suppression of the Learning Censor has become their forte, and the Learning Poet is left to lead the way in the darkness of a hostile culture. This, of course, is simply reversing the polarity.

The real issue here is one of how we can make use of each part of what might appear to be dichotomous mind functions without restricting the other. Function fragmentation and brain bias has become a life-style in our culture. Since researchers have been able to discover the dualities of mind functions using split-brain epileptics as research subjects, maybe it would be appropriate to say that the task ahead of us is to get our fit together.

6

Personal Meadows

We have mused a bit about a few of the realities of working with students of any age in virtually any educational setting. We've shared a sense that students possess bundles of talents to share and that only some of these talents are clearly valued by the dominant culture in our society. Some students come to us with talents most often considered threatening or undisciplined. And in other cases, the talents simply extend beyond our own perceptions and experiences.

We have briefly explored the impact of a very few but incredibly significant *men*. (I wonder what we could learn from that!) We have reflected on some of the ways in which we structure and view ourselves and our relationships with other human beings as a result of the gifts of these men. In particular we have touched on the ways these gifts of ideas affect those settings designated for teaching and learning.

We have been introduced to the Learning Censor and the Learning Poet. And we have wandered a bit to find their physiological relationship to ways of knowing in each of us. We have played with two-way rivers.

And now it is time to wonder, "Do I care?" If I am a teacher already, I have already made a commitment — and yet with each day I have more choices to make. I can continue to teach, I can walk more firmly in chosen paths, and I can explore new ones. I can also hitchhike if I choose. I can try to see a few new sights I like, and I can always decide to buy into a new mode of transportation. I can even forget the old and seek new journeys . . . the choice basically is always mine. I can dare to explore my *own* two-way river.

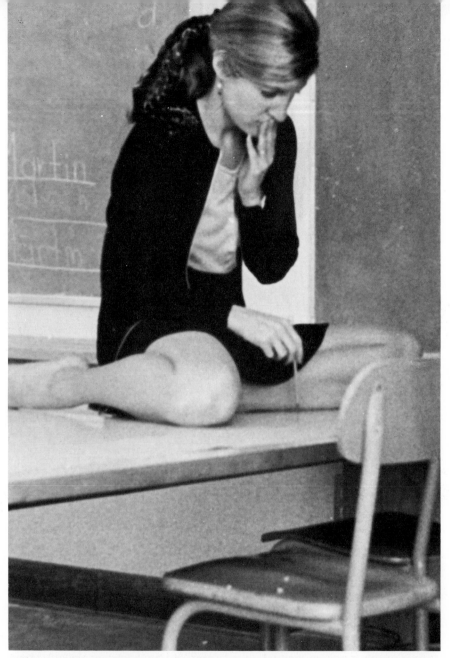

If I am just getting ready to teach for the first time, am thinking about or have already signed that first contract to teach, I have got choices to make too. If the contract is signed, I am pretty well committed, at least for this school year. If it is not, I have got plenty of time to get on a whole new wagon — maybe stock-broking, dental hygiene, or agribusiness are *really* more suited to my interests, capacities, and personality . . . for now, at least.

74

*I close my eyes . . . and take a deep breath.
I see myself walking some place I find
beautiful, restful. I walk a bit farther . . . and
I see some friends. I wave and go on.*

*Next I find myself engaged in some ac-
tivity I find genuinely exhilarating. I take the
time to experience it fully . . . and then I
pause to see clearly what it is I am doing.*

*With my eyes still closed, I take another
deep breath. I pause to reflect about my own
perception of my fantasy's accuracy. I reflect
to see if my fantasy of perfection is at all
related to what I am really doing with my
life.*

Now, just for fun, think for a moment about the compatibility of those things you find most exhilarating, exciting, nurturing in life — and think about their relationship to your activities as a teacher. If they aren't one in the same, or very much a part of each other, *might they by their differences each enrich the other?* That is, if your most favorite playtime has nothing to do with what might be your chosen worktime, teaching, could those playtime activities make you a more interesting and effective teacher? And could your worklife lend some enriching quality to your other pursuits?

MEMO

TO: ALL CERTIFIED PERSONNEL
FROM: DISTRICT OFFICE
RE: PROFESSIONALISM

It is important that all teachers present
a professional image to all who would observe
them. Planning and evaluating are an important part of ateachers job.Because these
responsibilities are so vital we will expect
teachers to carry them out each day between
the end of the last period and 3:45.

Leaving the school premises prior to that time
will be considered unprofessional behavior.

We know you will cooperate in this matter.

If you see nothing in common between those things you most like to do and what you see yourself doing as a teacher . . . and if you see no ways you could bring play and work together to enrich each other . . . IT MAY WELL BE THAT TEACHING IS NOT FOR YOU!

If you have been teaching for 17 years, it makes no difference — it still sounds like it's time for you to do something else! (Mortgage payments, hospital bills, and three kids in college might be relatively good reasons for sticking it out — but if so, it is time for you to get with making your "avocations" and "vocation" more harmonious!

And if you are not teaching yet, you can still carefully examine those things you like to do. If teaching doesn't seem to be one of them . . . you still have a chance to try a new course in your life. Don't teach . . . or check out what you perceive teaching to be. Whichever the case, it is time to begin to identify the things about your life that you like most. It is time to celebrate the differences you find, and it is time to bring the whole together in a life that brings you joy!

Remember, the greatest joy to a learner is to be in the presence of a person who truly wants to teach. If the teacher hates the scene, all that teacher can communicate to the learner is a confused message laden with hypocrisy and deceit.

To make the world a better place to live.●Learning's fun and I get as much kick out of it and learn as much as they do. ●Everyone in our family has always taught. ● I don't get along well with adults but I can handle kids.●It's a good steady job and the sum -mers are free.●I want to be with people who love me. ● There's something exquisite about the joy in a youthful face just struck with a magi- cal insight. ●Because it's fun ●I love kids. ● etc.

Activities

Use the following definitions in this activity:

    INTELLECTUALITY — the use of the mind in exploring life

    EMOTIONALITY — the use of feelings in exploring life

    SEXUALITY — the use of the body in exploring life

Motivation is related to each of these and though it is often difficult to separate them out, try to do it for this activity.

My motivation to teach is:

    (Example: INTELLECTUALITY — access to library

                   EMOTIONALITY — access to feeling people

                   SEXUALITY — access to free summers for hiking, etc.)

INTELLECTUALITY

EMOTIONALITY

SEXUALITY

In my non-teaching life I fulfill these wants by

INTELLECTUALITY

EMOTIONALITY

SEXUALITY

How do these lists match up?

me

I want to be me
. . .not a selfish me
so that I exploit you
for my own ends,
nor a selfless me,
a container that
constantly
pours out my being.

I want to be a me
who chooses to be with you
. . .to give
. . .receive
and sometimes just drift.

I want to be a me
that wants to be me
. . .as much
as I want you to be you.

Places Along the Way

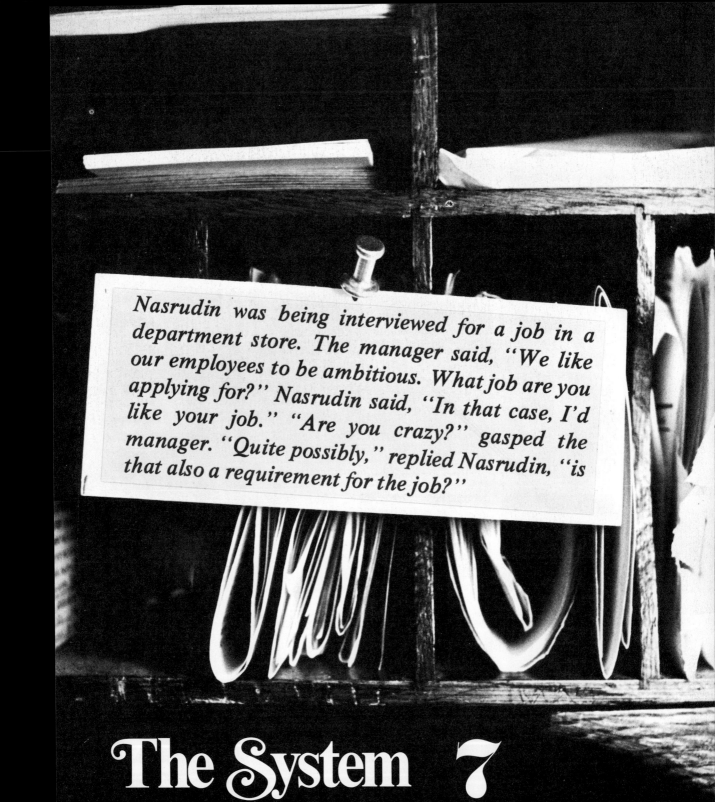

Nasrudin was being interviewed for a job in a department store. The manager said, "We like our employees to be ambitious. What job are you applying for?" Nasrudin said, "In that case, I'd like your job." "Are you crazy?" gasped the manager. "Quite possibly," replied Nasrudin, "is that also a requirement for the job?"

The System 7

The System. What is it? Who's in it? How does it work? How can it help? How can you use it? Can it use you? Where does the buck stop? Where does it start?

The "system" is supposed to be logical, ordered, classificatory, and tidy. It is not supposed to be metaphorical. So, first off, don't expect the "system" to run out seeking your new, fresh approach, and don't think it is waiting breathlessly to embrace your vision in regard to bringing about educational reform. It is not supposed to do that. The system is born of the left cerebral hemisphere. The system is the Learning Censor of education. Its function is to analyze, criticize, evaluate, justify, order, plan, verify, and be literal.

Sure, there have been attempts at changing systems, and some of them have succeeded. But even the changed ones are orderly, reasonable organizations that are interested in running smoothly "without rocking the boat."

The system is there to "keep track" and keep "on track." Sometimes it even builds new tracks, but they are still tracks. Don't expect the system to grow a meadow for you. When systems try to grow meadows, they seem to find it necessary to label all the plants and rocks and construct organized and planned nature trails. They are also compelled to have signs that say, "Stay on the trail." So the first job is not to fight it, but to know it. If there are going to be meadows in the system, they will have to be planted and grown by *you*. Don't go in thinking that they are already there or that it is the system's job to create them. It is up to *you*. Even from the start, the message gets through. Here is how it actually got started for one of the authors.

I drove into that little town and it seemed innocuous enough. The streets were clean and the buildings old but well cared for, at least here in the center of town where THE stop light flashed green and yellow and red eternally, its rhythm reflecting the pace of timeless life in rural America.

Riding with me was a primary school teacher candidate. As we both drove to this job interview, she nervously fixed her face, a task which should have taken no time at all, since she wore no makeup, a fact she had apologetically attributed to her religious background. But nonetheless she continued her "compactless" preening for so long that I was convinced she was about to perform her own version of a crash weekend at Elizabeth Arden's. She accompanied me to this interview simply because she needed a ride. I had received a phone call and a heartless voice on the other end said, "You wanted a science job, right?" The voice was familiar because it was the same voice that had announced a month earlier, "I'm sorry, you can't interview as a science teacher because you won't graduate with a science credential." I now wanted to be a science teacher. I had waited until my senior year to discover that fact. The voice had gone on, "With a physical education credential, you have to interview for physical education jobs." I tried to explain, "Except . . . I've changed my mind about wanting to teach phys. ed.," I had said. His face must have turned red. I could feel it and knew I was dead when he said, "Why don't you change majors then?" I was a senior and I had already done my student teaching, but I still had changed my mind. After an icy pause, the voice went on, "That's highly irregular, and in our system our procedures don't allow for that."

That was the end of the first phone call, and as far as I knew . . . my teaching career. But a couple of days later the voice called back. Now the voice was asking, "Do you have a car?" I stammered out, "Yes," which was not exactly true. What I really had was a brushpainted, fire-engine red, well-battered Plymouth with four doors and four speakers all held together by a dead battery. "Good," said the voice. "There are two job interviews at Glatchy Central School. One is for a primary school teacher and I've chosen a gal for that slot. She needs a ride." Then the voice paused . . . I waited and it finally added as an afterthought, "We are also interviewing for a secondary science teacher."

I almost asked the heartless voice if there was a hill on which I could park my four-door, four-speaker Plymouth with the dead battery. However, being resourceful, I reconsidered and decided to switch batteries with my roommate, who had a purple Ford with Hollywood mufflers and two flat tires.

So here we are. I made a sharp left and my passenger said, "Where are we going? The school's the other way." "I know," I said, "but we're early. Let's explore."

We drove around and looked at the town. We found that there were parts of town where the houses were old and not kept up. We also found some new houses going up in what had been a farmer's field. Most had three or four bedrooms. "Looks like a place for families. School population won't be getting smaller for a while." Of course that meant some job security, if you got tenure, as long as you didn't rape anybody. (Immorality is a lot easier to prove than incompetence.) It could also mean larger classes if there were no business or industrial reasons for these folks to move in. So we looked for the tax base. What were the industries? There was an old fruit-packing plant and two small machine industries. But apparently no new industry. As soon as we reached the town limits, we saw acres of fruit trees; the reason for the packing plant. Within these orchards we saw what looked like temporary buildings in which people were now obviously living. Migrant laborers! A transitory population that almost guarantees a teacher larger class loads for part of the year and extremely diverse educational backgrounds among the students. And perhaps racial prejudice and violence.

We drove back to town and stopped at the library. We pored over six months' worth of local weekly newspapers. The letters to the editor indicated that a vocal conservative group controlled most agricultural interests. The papers showed us that the school was very active in image building, since honor rolls, class activities, and merit scholars were highly visible. They told us that school sports were a major part of the community involvement and that winning was important. The baseball coach was "in" solid, having won last year's county championship and about to repeat. The soccer coach was also quite popular, until basketball season came around and his "so-so" record as basketball mentor put his winter solstice job in jeopardy.

The board of education's minutes indicated that the principal was well respected by board members and that they always rubber stamped his recommendations. There was a new member of the board, however, who seemed bent on making the school more "relevant."

My passenger and I each did our own private calculations of pluses and minuses and from our own vantages formed an image of the school we were about to see . . . then we saw it. It was basic worn-down. It was clean, somewhat repaired, and yet mildly frightening to both of us as we went in. We then parted. She went on to her elementary-level interview, which was held in this building. I was taken in tow by the senior high principal.

The principal was proud of "the plant," as he called it. I was given the grand whirlwind tour, interrupted only by a brief encounter with a student caught without a hall pass by my guide. The student quickly saw the logic of permission slips as this 6'3", 230-pound former athlete "held" the now-cowering student firmly against the tile wall while calmly asking to see the required pass. After falling short and being ordered to the office to wait, the student left us and we continued the tour. I was taken to the smoke-filled men's faculty room, and the silence which resulted from our entry was a deafening contrast to the jolly boisterousness I had heard through the closed door. I was introduced to the half-dozen faculty members in the room. There had been seven, but one had quickly extinguished a cigarette, forced a visit to the lavatory, and left. There were a few "hope you'll be able to join us!" 's and a couple of "yeah, misery loves company!" 's, and we left. I was not shown the women's faculty room, but was proudly told it was "new this year."

I was shown the science facilities and then given a five-minute interview with the science-department chairman. While speaking with the chairman, I became aggressively verbal, expressing interest in the possibility of field trips and the availability of lab space. Later, I wondered at the wisdom of this aggressiveness, but rationalized that appearing "innovative" would be less harmful to my chances than appearing ignorant in the face of possible questions the chairman couldn't ask if I talked instead.

I was then taken to the athletic director (the soccer and basketball coach), and he and I shared lunch with what turned out to be the entire coaching staff, which regularly gathered at noon in the director's office. The conversation centered on the star basketball player's possible probation due to academic deficiency. There were some interesting strategies invented for staving off what appeared to be the inevitable. But by the time I left, they had not yet figured out what to do about the boy's English grades. English, it seems, was a required course, and none of the coaches taught it.

I returned to the principal's office, where he and I chatted briefly about my impressions of "the plant." Then the principal leaned forward and asked in a hushed voice that he considered sincere, "Can you coach track?" I had been so immersed in the science possibility that I took a moment to regroup. Finally I stammered that my phys. ed. training prepared me to do so. "Well, good," the principal beamed, "if that's the case, we'd like to have you as part of our faculty." He placed in front of me a form which had a great deal of incomprehensible language on it . . . I was still stunned and signed in three places before I got the right line.

Later, I asked my passenger what our salaries would be, because I had forgotten to look on the contract. To my annoyance I discovered she had even read hers. We were so giddy we decided to stop for a drink to celebrate. Then I remembered and "suggested" that we wait until the next town, because the principal had made it clear that members of the school faculty usually did not frequent local taverns. We stopped at the first available out-of-our-new-town bar. Even the four-door, four-speaker, fire-engine red Ford-powered Plymouth seemed smugly pleased.

Activities

How not to take an interview . . .
   SERIOUSLY

Tips for getting that first job . . . or the one you'd really like to have:

Comb your hair or polish your bald spot. Dress neatly (tie your tie or clean your glasses). Get a good night's sleep (if they hire you it may be your last). Remember if you are new you may be viewed as a potential revolutionary. (Leave your armbands at home and take the bumper stickers off your car.)

Questions you may be asked at the interview:

- What's your philosophy of education?
- How do you feel about discipline?
- Would you be willing to supervise extracurricular activities?
- Would you be willing to team teach? (Not normally related to coaching students in competitive sports. On second thought, that can be the way it turns out!)
- What role do you think parents should have in setting school policy?

Answer each question above in two ways:
   1) fearful-timid
   2) arrogant-absurd

1. Jot the key words that seem to represent your philosophy of education.
2. Now make these words into a sentence, on this page.
3. Turn to page 197 for instructions in randomizing such a sentence.
4. Write your randomizing on this page too, complete with your new sentence.
5. Read what you've got. Terrific! Look what you know . . . that you didn't know you knew!

The system is here. There is no ignoring it. It will not go away if you close your eyes. Your school mailbox will still fill up with memos, survey forms, and announcements. The quietude of your classroom will be shattered by the P.A. system or the telephone. There will be calls for attendance, milk money, field-trip permission slips, standardized testing, textbook request forms. There will be teachers' organizations dues to pay, PTA meetings to attend, dances to chaperone, parents to appease, custodians to please, and cafeteria duty. There will be faculty meetings, curriculum meetings, evaluation meetings, and sometimes meetings of the mind. Your personnel file will grow as you exhibit your competence, incompetence, recalcitrance, decadence, and Merit Scholarship winners. You will be asked to prove that your students are learning so that the board of education will give you money. You'll be asked to prove that they are not learning so that the federal government will give you money. You'll be asked to convince an accreditation team that you are idealistic. You'll be asked to convince parents that you are pragmatic. You'll be asked to convince the state that you are not a Communist. You'll be expected to convince townspeople that you're not a Democrat (or Republican). You'll be expected through all of this not to be political, but to be economical, to be social (but within limits), to be scientific but not technical, to be humanistic but not personal, to be physical but not sexual, to be unprejudiced but discriminating, to be real but to play your role. Your creativity will be highly rewarded as long as it doesn't change anything. Your intellect will be admired as long as you can "keep it at the level of the everyday people." Adventuresomeness will be encouraged as long as you know its and your "place."

In short, the system will place you in an unending series of classic double binds, places where you will be asked to respond to two opposing value systems simultaneously. You will be asked to experience the conditions of schizophrenia and to emerge mentally healthy. Mental health will mean exhibiting appropriate behavior. And the norms are different for each situation. To be on the safe side — be mediocre in all that you do. This is the system's message. This is also the system's legitimate function. The system will never fire you for being mediocre. It can't. The rest of the system will not allow that, because that would be a radical departure from former practice, and the system is built to guard against radical departures of any sort.

BUT WAIT A MINUTE! You say that the system can't be all that bad?

We never said it was bad. We only said that is the way it works. Systems are not good or bad. They are just systems. Some things that *happen* in systems are good, some are bad, and lots of them just "are." But the system doesn't judge that. The slots and channels don't judge anything. The *people* who fill the slots and swim the channels make those judgments. After all, education is a human enterprise. It is humans who have invented good and bad, love and hate, right and wrong, right and left. And because human beings have invented these things, they change. The system goes on. It continues to say "hold it!" when change begins. But the human beings filling the slots keep kicking the system. They kick it not so the system will change, but so that one of the human beings in the system will say "ouch" and pay attention. It is like the person who kicks the door that won't shut. The door isn't going to get better by itself. The house won't get up and move to a warm climate where it won't need doors. But if one kicks hard enough, the alert household repair person might hear the commotion and come and fix the door just to quiet things down. Problems occur, of course, if there is no competent, handy, fix-it person around the house. But that is not the house's fault. Then everybody just gets in the habit of kicking the door.

CONVERSATION OVERHEARD IN A TEACHER'S LOUNGE:

Teacher A: What we need is a political system that's responsive to the people.
Teacher B: What kind of a system do you suggest?
A: Benevolent dictatorship. That's the only way. Let one kind, competent, responsible person make the rules and everybody follow them.
B: Dictatorship! I'll be damned if I'd live in a dictatorship. Ours may not be the best system possible, but it's better than any other one around.
A: But it's no damned good.
B: It may not be perfect, but it's what makes it possible for you and me to be here.
A: Don't you think a benevolent dictator would let you teach?
B: I didn't say that. But a dictator would take your money, tax hell out of your property, we'd have corruption and graft in government and business. You see it all the time in those foreign countries.
A: Sounds like home to me.
Teacher C: How about a responsible anarchy?
A and B: Anarchy! You can't have anarchy. You'd have crime in the streets and chaos.
C: Sounds like home to me. Besides, I said *responsible* anarchy. As long as we're inventing utopias that will never happen, let's invent one that puts the burden where it belongs.
BELL RINGS.
A, B, and C: Goddamned bell. I'm gonna tear it out of the wall one of these days. I gotta get to class. The district wants those damned standardized tests given today. Next year I'm gonna refuse to do it. If they want those things given, let 'em come down here and give them themselves.

We can believe that the system is real and bad and try to operate outside of it. In that case, it is controlling us as much as if we believed it to be good. We're still reacting to the system, still part of it, even though we are no longer in it.

Someone asked Nasrudin, "Is kebab with an <u>a</u> or an <u>o</u> ?"   "With meat," he replied.

Positive Coping With(in) the System
Don't *own* the system. It's not *all* your problem.

Don't let it own you.

Remember when you close the classroom door *you and the students* own the setting.

It isn't all good. It isn't all bad.

But in most cases, life within its parameters can be productive and healthy. And yes, we believe you *can* make a difference.

Be careful about being a visionary in the teacher's lounge and a totalitarian in the classroom.

CHECK LIST FOR POSITIVE COPING WITH(IN) THE SYSTEM
- sense of humor
- flexibility
- competence (remember these three?)
- assertive capacity
- grace
- good running shoes
- sense of humor (yes, we said it again!)
- (add your own based on personal style . . .)
-
-
-
-

INTERVIEWER: Describe the ideal system worker.

PERFECT SYSTEM: They are all perfect in a sense. That is, they all fulfill a function to make schools what they are. But if you are asking for utopia, one that takes into account the community's interests and values but still runs efficiently **and** effectively, there is a certain kind of person who fits that description better than others. That person is the one who understands how the system works but also realizes it is of minor importance. That person seldom seriously complains about the system unless realistically convinced that it can be changed **and** that the effort is worth it. But workers find out what the system can do for them and they let the system do it. They also find out what systems **cannot** do for them and they do that for themselves. Workers in the perfect system realize that systems can seldom harm them unless they try to force specific values on the system — values that are really not the community's. They also realize that systems have too much else to do to insist on more than a superficial dealing with community values. I'd say that these magic people are **in** systems but not **of** systems. I guess they are the ones who really understand that systems are there to provide a service. If that service is useful to the workers, the workers use the system. If not, they humor the system. And given a chance, they even enjoy sitting down and engaging in mutual therapy by trying to change things. This is all in good humor, but no one has grandiose expectations. Many of those who really affect systems are slightly subversive. They become change agents in the classrooms and in the offices. They don't stand on street corners shouting at passersby. Zealots are terrible agents for changing systems. The **real** agents of transformation in the culture don't waste energy. They know the difference between weapons and tools.

One evening Nasrudin said to his wife, "Bring some cheese to eat, for cheese enhances the appetite and makes the eyes bright."

"We are out of cheese," the wife said.

"That is good," Mulla replied, "for cheese is injurious to the teeth and gums."

"Which of your statements is then true?" she asked.

Nasrudin answered, "If there is cheese in the house, the first; if not, the second."

this is sloppy work... I will subtract 20 points for this. Watch this next time!

The Building 8

The best of school buildings are places where "building" takes place. That is, places for establishing foundation and celebrating growth. For too long at least one other alternative has been dominant. School buildings have been places in which things are *kept*. They have been warehouses of humans, of books, of desks, and of materials protected from access to the outside world. Sequestered without light, this vision of school buildings has created museums isolated from the culture at large. Such buildings have become places where no healthy growth can take place.

You will be most likely to find *some* kind of "building" in your role as a teacher.

You will have a major role in determining what kind of "building" will take place in your building.

Or perhaps a better way would be to think of what kind of *growth* you will nurture in your building.

Who said a school can't be a garden?

Draw the floor plan of your school. (If you aren't presently teaching, draw one you know a lot about.) Include the school grounds in your layout. Indicate the general purpose of each area you designate; for example: classrooms, principal's office, laboratories, lavatories, library . . .)

Map the people patterns:

- places where hardly anything *grows*
- places with the best nutrients for growth
- places you feel groovy
- places where the minimum of cultivation will make things grow better
- places where more cultivation than you have time for would be needed
- places where learning poets live . . . where learning censors live
- places Freud . . . Skinner . . . Piaget . . . etc. would like.

On the map you drew indicate the locations of friends, enemies and neutrals.

Do a role check. Is your "friend" list made up only of those whose roles are the same as yours? . . . Are enemies those whose roles differ?

This all sounds kind of like a military action plan, so let's go on.

Plan a peace conference.

Since *they* don't know there is an action plan, make the plan only for yourself.

Many people in the Building are frequently forgotten. Their talents for lending grace and wisdom to the process of teaching and learning are sometimes neglected. And not all the *places* for teaching and learning are discovered or in use on *every* school campus. In the pages that follow, we'll explore a few of the special people *and* places sometimes forgotten or unnoticed.

Preschools, elementary schools, intermediate schools, and high schools usually have at least one (maybe more!) *secretary*. All stereotypes included, secretaries are usually very special people. They really *do* have access to the principal, custodial staff, board of education, and the PTA.

Know that secretaries are special, know that they deserve respect for a variety of reasons . . . certainly because any human does, certainly because your job as a teacher will be more rewarding and fun if your relationships throughout the school community are warm and amicable, and certainly because it is incredible the MAGIC these people can work!

Secretaries in any organization are the focal point of all communication. They are the facilitators of all the information flow. They expose or protect the principal, the teachers, and the students. If a school has a reputation for being humane, it is as much a function of the secretary as it is of the teachers and administration. The life of a school secretary, like that of any school person, is one of interruptions and sudden shifts in direction. Yet by the very nature of the position, the secretary's clientele is much more varied than most. The school secretary is like the central part of a flower whose petals reach in all directions. All things touch base with this center.

Your paycheck is lost. The payroll office is closed. The SECRETARY calls and the payroll manager writes you a check out of special emergency funds.

Your mother broke her leg; your dad is out of town. The SECRETARY says, "Go ahead — Mary Green can cover your class for an hour. By then, I'll have a substitute here."

It's 7:30 A.M. School hasn't started yet. You've got this great idea to improve next semester's social studies program. You just need this one set of materials — some supplementary books of readings the publisher's rep showed you last week. The department chairperson's out of money — the principal's got a few hundred dollars left in a special fund for Curriculum Enrichment . . . but the principal's always so busy! You've been trying to get in to see her in her office for weeks. "Just a second," says the principal's SECRETARY. The SECRETARY taps softly on the principal's office, fresh cup of coffee in hand, slips in the office, slips out again (without the coffee), and says, "Go right on in — the principal can talk to you now."

secretaries teach

Who can find 12 extra chairs for Open House when no one else can?

Who can get the purple paint spilled on the floor off the floor in time for Open House that same night?

Who just smiles and hides the "evidence" when your classroom has an inch of sawdust all over the floor every night for a week — and you don't teach woodshop?!

Who can brighten the dreariest moment when it's 6:30 P.M., you're still at your desk, you're surrounded by stacks and stacks of student records and "contracted study" projects . . . and you hear a voice say, "Tough day, huh!"

But be ready . . . if you turn into a self-centered, arrogant, degreed missionary of some high educational cause, there just might be a custodian there to close every door and make your life a living terror. Everyone in any school is important. Roles do not make the person . . . the person makes the role. Custodians are vital resources as well as vital colleagues. If invited to, each can provide experiences and insights for students and teachers that are not available elsewhere.

custodians teach

Activities

Each person in the school is a resource. Yet all have roles. Find out how you can celebrate each person's presence *and* how you can become part of *their* celebration.

Tap each person's talents informally or formally. Sometimes *Talent Directories* work, with everyone in a school listing by their names the talents and time they'd be willing to share with others. That includes Mr. Gray's 5th grade class tutoring Mrs. White's second graders in addition and subtraction skills. It also includes Mr. Moustache, the principal, sharing the process of making butter. (He used to live on a farm!)

Now find out how you can make a support-based offering for each person's role. Determine how teachers and students can facilitate the roles of others. All of this is related to lowering the de-humanizing elements and elevating the humanizing qualities in each school building.

Everything you've heard is probably ...TRUE

They do exist. And sometimes there really *are* Men's Lounges and Women's Lounges. And very *infrequently* there are Student's Lounges.

They're a place to put up your feet, relax, laugh, eat a banana, and — sometimes — smoke a cigarette.

They're a place to *hear gossip* (if you don't indulge), to *hear silence* if you tell everyone else there to lay off the gossip, to *hear complaints* . . . complaints about the kids, the principal, the kids, the budget, the kids, the superintendent, the kids, their parents, the kids, any other teacher not in the lounge, the kids.

And, on special occasions, to have a good time.

"Who's takin' this stuff seriously — teachin' I mean?" asks a voice. "We are!" laughs the chorus.

An old claim holds that the teachers' lounges are where most of the zealots make their speeches. Being a change agent in the teacher's lounge is easier than in the classroom. But regardless what happens in them, they are an eddy in the flow of school. A place to go to get a change of pace. Like any other place in life, they become what you want them to be.

THERE ARE MOST ALWAYS ATHLETIC FACILITIES ON SCHOOL
GROUNDS NEAR BUILDINGS . . . .

Keep in mind in these days of less exercise and more need . . . there are
places . . . usually on any school grounds . . . to (do ten pushups immediately
to convince me you're HEALTHY if it hurts you to *hear* this!) . . . EXERCISE!
Shoot baskets — run a lap. Swim 200 breaths worth. Do it alone or with a
teacher, a student, a parent, a . . . .

They exist, they're frequently used for *competitive sports* — and that's okay if
you like to compete or watch other folks do it . . . BUT THERE ARE SOME
OTHER CHOICES!

You don't have to be on the NEW GAMES mailing list to know you can get
out there on the field, alone or with friends, and engage in some good, healthy,
and fun physical exercise . . . stuff that your principal and your students' parents

AND THERE ARE *HIDING* PLACES . . . .

The one significant thing to remember about hiding places is that *every* school has them. And if you, the teacher, seek them out . . . you can be pretty sure that students do too.

For fun, and to keep you sensitive . . . CHECK THEM OUT . . . *Without necessarily interfering!* (How would you like it if someone took *yours* away — given that in your hiding place you weren't molesting guinea pigs, putting arsenic in plant-food containers, or tearing pages out of required math textbooks!)

SOME HIDING PLACES (Most of these are well known or we wouldn't share them!)

- behind and under the branches of any large trees at the far end of the school grounds
- on the drinking-fountain side of the handball courts (facing the street and not the school buildings)
- in the girls' restroom*
- in the boys' restroom*
- in the far corner of the school cafeteria *before* school starts
- in the back of any bus, any time there's access
- (fill in the ones you spot!)

If school *is* a garden, find out where each creature would hide. Rabbits, snails, birds, worms, etc.

*Note how difficult it is for *students* to find pleasant, harmless hiding places. It might surprise many new teachers and some experienced ones to find out that some school districts make it a policy to guarantee spaces for student privacy. Dividers and partitions are placed in some cafeterias and libraries. Classrooms often have screens or curtained-off areas that are reserved for student use.

9

The Room

Where does it all happen?

There's a place — a place where people come together in some way to share learning.

Sometimes it's a single room, sometimes a corner in a huge open space, sometimes a scrap of grass with shade near a dusty sidewalk. Maybe your room is a 14-foot tall, echoing chamber of wood and plaster built at the turn of the century. Maybe dust drifts across sun rays and is swirled by breezes that slip in cracks that are icy in November.

But whatever it is like, it is the place — the place for sort of "centering." And it's *yours*.

So too is it *theirs*. It belongs to whoever gathers there with that common purpose . . . to learn, to be stimulated, to grow, to expand and extend growing awarenesses, understandings, skills, and bases of knowledge.

No matter what the place, no matter what the age of those who will gather there, if the purpose has been established . . . and it is that people will each learn (or *have* each learned — it's fair to discover that afterwards!) . . . there is one common and identifiable characteristic.

THE ENVIRONMENT IS MEANINGFUL TO EACH PERSON GATHERED THERE!

What we mean by this is that for real learning to take place, any person there must be *involved*, must be *interested*, must somehow *be engaged in the act of being there*. The room will house what happens. It will become an extension of all those within it. The environment might simply be represented by one person's interaction with personal thought processes in a quiet setting — or might be a group of people in animated and stimulating discussion, oblivious to exterior and inanimate elements around them — or might be any number of people excitedly engaged in play with the parts of a physically rich and abundant setting.

No matter what the specific setting, the learner must be engaged — engaged with what we call an attitude to learn.

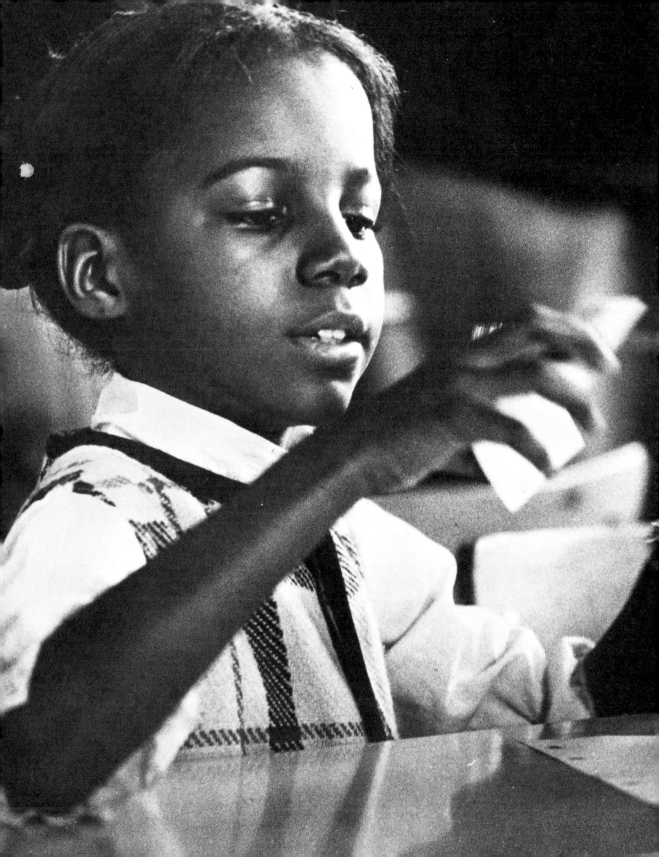

A *SOMETIMES* STATEMENT . . .

"If the exterior environment is important to the student, it ought to be rich."

Rich doesn't have to look rich.
To look rich is sometimes to be too rich to learn.
But not to look rich *and* not to be rich is not rich enough to learn.

The richness of the classroom is as much an attitude as it is anything. Too often adults turn the classroom into a vision of themselves. Students enter the room and find an exaggeration of the teacher's personality. At the very start this excludes them from doing much more than fitting in! The whole environment becomes a kind of loaded mousetrap in which all the moves are called by someone other than the students. What they learn in such places is how to psych out the teacher. They also learn how to conform. If they don't, their only choice is to rebel. And we all know how that turns out.

In classrooms where shared celebration occurs, the place belongs to everyone. Students own it as well as does the teacher. Stuff is everywhere and is used. The bulletin boards, graffiti corners, interest centers, and plants belong to all. Books are used and pictures are looked at. Sometimes floors are walked on, but other times they become places to sit, lie, or work. The out-of-doors is fair ground, as it and the rest of the world are considered to be an extension of this learning place.

The living classroom is not a postponed experience. Learning moves outward and inward like each breath each person takes. Everything becomes a tool for further exploration. Silence as well as noise is common. Each person is respected, as is the group. Materials and equipment vary, but one thing that remains basic is the worth of each person. The worth underlies the whole process of learning.

If learners are deeply engaged in some reverie or thinking process within themselves — oblivious to exterior realities — the exterior environment doesn't much matter . . . except that it shouldn't *interfere*.

But much of the time we as learners are open to stimulation from our exterior environment. And most often public schools do not take effective advantage of this reality . . . are not sensitive enough to the composition of learning environments . . . are not aware enough of what exists . . . what probably shouldn't be . . . and what *could* be in order for learning to be celebrated!

Activities

CHECKLIST TO FIND OUT IF YOUR ROOM IS A PLACE WHERE LEAR-
NING IS CELEBRATED!

- varied materials are available to be explored
- **student**-created products are in evidence
- teacher looks interested
- students look interested
- lots of teacher and student "movement"
- student-**initiated** activities and products are common
- resources are available to extend and expand exploration
- ready access is available to people and things **outside** of
  the classroom and school grounds
- ready access is available to people and things **inside** of
  the school but outside of the classroom
- respect for human beings and personal property is
  evident

In schools a great deal of confusion exists in regard to what an educational setting is. Some people focus on curriculum. Others on management. Of course the real answer is that both are deeply interrelated. What follows is a description of rooms . . . or ways that rooms reflect the curriculum and educational setting.

What we're calling rooms — the places where education takes place — affect the quality of what goes on within them. The actual physical setting can have an impact. Many people feel that students can pay attention more readily in what might be called "sterile" settings. Some school managers have even removed windows from classrooms in order to lower the number of distractions. Others have created rooms that are carnivals of distractions. We favor a third category among these extremes which, for lack of a better word, can be called "seductive."

The seductive classroom is neither austere nor distracting. It is rich. It is full of things that beg for attention but still can be synchronized into learning sequences. It is a room where the curriculum is not only interesting, but also well supported by materials and options available to the students.

Such rooms, magic when they are found, are often victims of certain educational-management strategies. For example, the "room" is not the same at all levels of schooling. Elementary school rooms are *different* from secondary. The patterns of rooms, students, and teachers vary. On the next few pages, the most common variations on the "room" will be explored. Keep in mind that each model of management affects the whole ecology in which learning takes place. Keep in mind too that often in education, innovation has been equated with a change in the way spaces, materials, and students are interrelated. Each of these changes has had certain consequences.

CONVENTIONAL FOUR WALLS, SELF-CONTAINED

A perennial favorite, this classic classroom setting has much to commend it. It lost some favor during the last decade, but its popularity is on the increase again in many communities. (In many, to be sure, it never went out of favor!) A strong feature of such classrooms can be the personal and homey environment that is sometimes created. Also there is continued access over time to the resources within by the same group of students and teachers (usually just one teacher in this setting). A continuity and naturalness can typify the characteristics contributing to the effectiveness of this setting. Privacy — with room to risk — can dwell within these walls. Students usually spend the entire school day within this space, moving out for field trips — and on most days — recess, lunch, often P.E., and, sometimes, but not always, art and music.

Grade Level: usually elementary; almost never secondary.

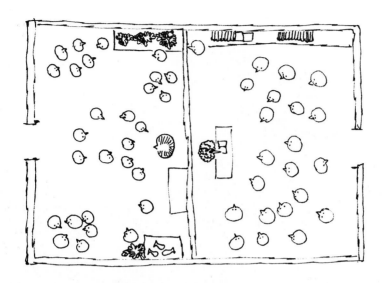

FOUR WALL SELF CONTAINED

- It can be decorated.
- It can be left "as is" when projects are underway.
- It can be made homelike.
- There is a sense of continuity.
- There is a sense of ownership.
- A community tends to emerge.
- Identity with a territory emerges.
- Isolation can occur.
- If the teacher is magic, so too will the room be. (**But** if not
  . . .)
- It can be changed without affecting others.
- A single philosophy dominates.
- Individual attention is usually easier.
- No one else's schedules need to be consulted.
- Field trips are easier as no other classes are affected.
- A better sense of knowing parents, families, etc., tends to
  emerge.

The Action:
You've just been *assigned* to teach in a "conventional, four walls, self-contained" classroom. You've been assigned to teach the _____ grade (you fill in).

In the space below, based on your own analysis of your style as a teacher, identify the things you think you *can* do . . . and things you think you *can't* do in this setting.

Invent three ways to do any one of the things you think you can't.

OPEN SPACE, WITH LEARNING CENTERS

This new favorite of many has gained special favor in recent years, playing for many teachers and students the hero's role in "saving" the kids from the constraints often attributed to the self-contained classroom just described. In its glory, the open-spaced classroom is characterized by a large open area with brightly colored carpet or rugs (to reduce noise level with so much traffic involved) filled with clusters of tables and chairs arranged throughout the room with space in between for easy traffic flow. Many of the clusters of tables and chairs are designed around some engaging display — science equipment, animals, plants, puppets, reading materials, tape recorders, and sound equipment. It is common for three or four teachers to share this space with approximately 30 students each, equalling about 90 to 120 students. Some private space is a necessity in these settings. This quiet and private space can be created in many ways. For example, a corner of the room may be draped with curtains hung from the ceiling or over large boxes. The curtains then make walls with a cosy couch and pillows inside. (Not always a panacea, as you can imagine if you let your imaginations wander!)

Each of the teachers usually has a space to meet regularly with an assigned one third or one fourth of the students in a sort of "home base." Students may spend all day, one-half day, or a few-hour block of time in this setting. It often depends on the grade levels and the number of teachers involved.

Grade Level: K-12; elementary-age students tend to spend more time in these settings, again leaving for recess, P.E., lunch, sometimes music, sometimes art. Secondary teachers have in recent years adopted use of this setting, typically combining two or more teachers with a large group of students for a few-hour block of time in some sort of interdisciplinary studies program. Example: one English and one American history teacher meet with 70 students for two hours in what is called an American Studies program.

122

OPEN SPACE

- Interaction with others teachers is high.
- More planning and coordination are typically required than in other settings.
- Materials and resources are often pooled.
- Can be noisy.
- Discipline can be a greater responsibility.
- Higher amount of student freedom often characterizes this setting.
- There is more probability for independent study by students to be encouraged.
- There is more efficient use of films because of larger groups.
- Transdisciplinary approach to content can easily be nurtured.
- Large- and small-group options encourage choice making.
- Teacher personalities are important.
- There is high peer exposure for both teachers and students.
- More teacher and student movement is typical.
- The environment is changeable, responsive to the number of different people affecting it.
- Students can see adults working together.
- Students can acquire large-group skills.
- Time can be more flexible.

CAUTION: Few teachers today have spent time as *students* in such settings. Some would call this "good." Others "bad." But many are not yet comfortable in celebrating the positive features of such settings — much less finding them! Instead, teachers find themselves bogging down (sometimes literally!) in the number of students and the logistical problems inherent. Chaos of the unpleasant sort frequently ensues. At the *secondary* level, frequent problems are overly enthusiastic architects, boards of education, and administrators who foist such gloriously "innovative" settings on a community, only to find they don't have enough teachers who really *want to teach in them!* Moreover, few teachers have enough experience to feel competent in doing so. Elementary teachers have done more of the kind of teaching that accompanies open-space settings in their self-contained classrooms for years. After all, you've got to have some things going for you if you stay locked up in one room all day with a bunch of "ankle biters!" But secondary teachers are sometimes unprepared to go "public" all of a sudden. Few are used to having their peers right there with them to see what's happening *all* the time. In addition, they are suddenly teaching *more* students for *longer* periods of time. All are engaged in a setting and style of teaching almost completely foreign to them!

RESULT: Backlash in some places. "Temporary" walls are becoming permanent; open spaces are "closing" and fast resembling self-contained classrooms, except with far poorer acoustics. Noise and lack of privacy are the architectural traps that ensnare those who come up with containers before attitudes are considered.

IMPLICATION: Someone *can* build a better mousetrap — but who gets caught?!

124

Activities

The Action:
You've just been *assigned* to teach in an "open space" classroom. You've
been assigned to teach the _____ grade (you fill in).

In the space below, based on your own analysis of your style as a teacher, identify the things you think you *can* do . . . and things you think you *can't* do in this setting.

Invent three ways to do any one of the things you think you can't.

FOUR WALLS, STUDENT MIGRATION

- Specialized content instruction is typical.
- Instructional materials can be rich and organized, located in one setting throughout each day.
- Settings can be consistent with specific content.
- Specialization of teachers is encouraged.
- Provides a "break" for students; gives them a variety of experiences with teachers.
- Requires management in scheduling.
- Field trips are more difficult to schedule.
- Frequent interruption of significant learning, as the "bell rings."
- Environment can reflect teacher's identity.

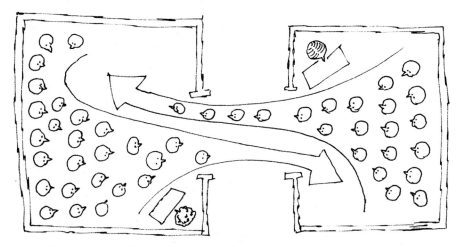

CONVENTIONAL FOUR WALLS; STUDENTS ON TREASURE HUNT

This setting is much like the *first* one described, except that students typically spend each class period a day in a series of these rooms. Teachers often spend all day (with time out for planning, lunch, and ground duty!) in this same four-walled setting. A striking feature of this setting is the teacher's "control" over the environment. Some teachers get to spend literally years in the same setting, building a wealth of resources and creating an inviting and enriched home into which students are invited one period each day, with brief visits sometimes welcomed before and after school. Special places these, with the turned-on and talented teacher. A student is lucky to find *one* of these stand-out rooms (with a teacher) in any given school year.

Grade Level: typically secondary, with an increased move toward use of this setting at the elementary (particularly upper) grade levels.

126

Activities

The Action:
You've just been *assigned* to teach in a "four walls, student migration" classroom. You've been assigned to teach the _____ grade (you fill in).

In the space below, based on your own analysis of your style as a teacher, identify the things you think you *can* do . . . and things you think you *can't* do in this setting.

Invent three ways to do any one of the things you think you can't.

FOUR WALLS, EVERYONE MIGRATING

- Specialized content instruction is typical.
- Requires significant management to schedule.
- Materials are difficult to deploy.
- Cuts down on out-of-school flexibility.
- Field trips can be difficult.
- Helps students prepare for impermanence in real life.
- Frequent interruptions of significant learning and overall superficiality of learning encouraged by transience can be a problem.

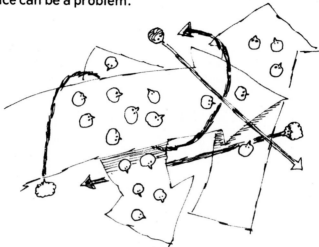

CONVENTIONAL FOUR WALLS; STUDENTS AND TEACHER ON TREASURE HUNT

A relatively new phenomenon, this setting finds both the students and the teachers changing location from period to period. The students we can understand perhaps — but why the teachers? Sometimes it's because the teachers are teaching various *different* subjects, requiring different equipment in different settings. That might be reasonable if the teacher teaches three periods of American history in a conventional four-walled setting with rich, varied, and appropriate support materials; then moves to a science lab for two periods of environmental problems (team-taught with a biology teacher); and then after school to the athletic department to coach interscholastic golf.

HOWEVER, there is a growing trend, especially at those secondary schools just recovering from aborted attempts to use open-spaced settings effectively, to shuttle teachers about from space to space throughout the day, teaching one different elective after another in sterile, four-walled ("temporary" but permanent) settings with no in-residence resources at all.

Grade Level: most often secondary.

Activities

The Action:
You've just been assigned to teach in a "four walls, everyone migrates"
classroom. You've been assigned to teach the _____ grade (you fill in).

In the space below, based on your own analysis of your style as a teacher,
identify the things you think you *can* do . . . and things you think you *can't* do in
this setting.

Invent three ways to do any one of the things you think you can't.

NO WALLS, STREET LEARNING APPROACH

- A high sense of real involvement is characteristic.
- Can be difficult to schedule.
- There are usually problems in evaluation.
- Great breadth in experience is provided both teachers and students.
- High student and teacher interaction.
- Long-lasting personal relationships tend to develop.

NO WALLS, STREET-LEARNING APPROACH

Popularized during the 1960's, this approach to learning settings was a matter of taking "to the streets." Kids found their way, with and without teachers, to folks in their communities. They worked at the side of carpenters, doctors, lawyers, mechanics, and factory workers. They visited City Hall not just once, but every day for three weeks to sense that kind of immersion in political action that public life brings. Contrary to some popular mythology, the kids weren't really alone and on the street — they typically met regularly in stable and small groups with the same teacher or teachers over a period of time. Sometimes they would use a teacher's home as a base from which to explore their community; other times a "bona fide" office would be established. But the overall thrust was legitimately to involve the students in what they and the teachers and their parents felt were meaningful learning experiences in daily contact with what they called "the real world."

Grade Level: K-12; most popular from intermediate grades up.

NOTE: These settings are dwindling in number today, but have had considerable impact on the "consciousness" of those concerned with American education today.

RESULT: Not just attributed to this movement, but still related . . . note how many "mainstream" schools allow students to develop programs of meaningful involvement within their communities. For example: work-study and intern programs, particularly at the secondary level. Another example: continued and increasingly more meaningful and regular involvement of community members in actual classroom activities on school sites.

Activities

The Action:

You've just signed a contract to teach in a "no walls, street learning" classroom. (People are hardly *ever* *assigned* to teach in such settings!) You've contracted to teach the _____ grade (you fill in).

In the space below, based on your own analysis of your style as a teacher, identify the things you think you *can* do . . . and things you think you *can't* do in this setting.

Invent three ways to do any one of the things you think you can't.

In the pages preceding, you should have been able to identify your own strengths and weaknesses (as you perceive them) in the face of teaching in a specified setting. That analysis can be terrifically useful to you — since sometimes such teaching *assignments* are actually made by those in a position to hire. Sometimes too, simply because you really want to teach — you'll take an assignment that puts you in a setting you might not normally have chosen. In any case, you end up facing the challenge of making the best of it!

CONVENTIONAL FOUR WALLS	OPEN SPACE	FOUR WALLS, STUDENT MIGRATION	FOUR WALLS, EVERYONE MIGRATES	NO WALLS

Fill in the Blank with the
Classroom Setting most
appropriate to do the following:

ACTIVITY

Check here if this is an
ACTIVITY YOU VALUE

EXAMPLE:
Teacher can hide from principal.

Teachers are never evaluated by administrators.
Kids can laugh during reading time.
Paint can spill on the floor.
There is a place to meditate.
A lot of things can be done without getting permission.
Lectures are appropriate.
Students can share in decision-making.
I don't have to put everything away.
I can eat and drink anything I want to in public.
Folks from the community can visit.
Other teachers can watch what I do.
I can visit other classrooms in progress.

Sometimes numerical analysis can be helpful.

This may not be one of those times . . . but look to see if your check ✔ marks
indicate that you have a preference for any particular classroom setting.

133

Despite how useful the analysis you've just made can be . . . we have the following to say. You can have open education in a closet, be a dictator in Outward Bound — and if there are puddles on the floor you can float boats on them or cry and add to the water supply. A room can reflect your attitude — or get in your way . . . be an expression of what you are — or a scapegoat for what you aren't! You decide.

to teach is to celebrate
to live is to celebrate
to love is to celebrate
to work is to celebrate
to cry is to celebrate
to laugh is to celebrate
to help is to celebrate
to be helped is to celebrate
to transform is to celebrate
to teach is to laugh is to cel
to live is to celebrate
to cry is to celebrate
to love is to celebrate
to help is to
to wor to be

Weeds, Seeds, and Gardens

10

Weeds and Other Living Things

A weed is anything alive and growing which you do not like.

There are no weeds in a meadow.

Gardens do have weeds, as do cornfields and lawns. But gardens, cornfields, and lawns are all imposed conditions on what would be an otherwise spontaneous ecology. In gardens, cornfields, and lawns we are compelled to pull the weeds. Or as is becoming more popular, to spray them with stuff that kills everything in sight. In meadows it is sometimes difficult to tell what is a weed and what is not, so we are less compelled to pull the weeds and more inclined to view the meadow as a place where weeds and nonweeds coexist, each contributing to the meadow's ecology. Only in imposed ecologies do weeds exist, and then only by definitions based on preconceived notions of what the ecology should be like.

School is kind of like that. There are some things and situations that can be viewed as nuisances, or worse. We can call those weeds. Yet they do exist. If we pull a weed, we often find another growing in its place in a short time. If we allow the weeds to coexist with the nonweeds, we can often enrich the ecology. The problem comes from defining and judging weeds. In any case, they must be attended to, or accepted.

EASY WEEDING

I have a small bank by my road which used to have alder trees growing on it. These were cut down. There were many plants which took over once the trees were cut. Most of them could be described as weeds. For a while I tried to pull the weeds and keep the bank neat. Soon it became obvious, however, that this was a full-time task and doomed to failure. Weeds grow very fast. Finally, after attempts at just cutting back the weeds periodically, I was called away for a year. When I returned, I noticed that some small alder trees were growing among the weeds. I didn't get around to cutting the weeds and the alder trees got bigger. After a while I found that only certain kinds of weeds were growing with the trees. Later, when the trees got quite large, I noticed that beneath the trees, on the bank where all the weeds had grown, there were no more weeds. The bank had weeded itself.

Some Common Weeds

If you survey a group of teachers, many of them would say,

"Weed Rather Not":

take attendance

make out report cards

collect milk money

teach "slow kids"

give standardized tests

have open house

have hall duty

have playground duty

have to get permission

fill out administrative forms

respond to surveys

generate budgets

chaperone

go to faculty meetings

attend PTA

police the lavatories

List your own favorite weeds:

Of course, other teachers and some administrators see many of these items not as weeds, but as important "processes" necessary to cultivate, irrigate, fertilize, and weed the garden. So perceptions do have something to do with identifying weeds. Your own list is, of course, the important one for you. It's the one which will identify the source of your tension headaches, your drained feeling after school and on weekends, your bursts of anger in the faculty lounge, and your feelings of helplessness which appear periodically. They are the source, not the cause. If they were the cause, everyone would have the same symptoms from the same source. Obviously some people really get off on policing the lavatories.

In this chapter we are taking a look at some of these weeds from the view that something can be done to make them easier to live with. We can't promise you the universal herbicide, but we hope we'll give you something to mulch on.

Stress is one of the most aggravating of all weeds. It pops up and grows in all the corners of your psyche without regard to how experienced you are. Strangely, very young people and more aged people seem not to be too bothered by this weed, as they seem to know how to ignore it and do things that are more productive. The rest of us often get caught up in the nettles of stress. Stress consumes an awesome amount of energy. And stress is a constant companion in the gardens of education.

Stress appears in classrooms with great frequency. At least one researcher describes teaching as being second only to the work of air traffic controllers for the stress typically accompanying the role.

"Who was the vice-president under Harry Truman, Miss Green?"

Miss Green, suddenly that color as well as that name, draws momentarily blank. For some people, this would constitute no stress at all. She, however, is one of the many who can't say (or even think about saying) the following without great knots bulging uncomfortably in her stomach:

"I don't know — well, at least I don't remember right this minute!" She says this softly, obviously uptight about it, to the student who asked.

"HEY!!!" The student says this LOUDLY so most of the rest of the students look up with a start! "HEY! MISS GREEN DOESN'T KNOW! DOESN'T KNOW THE ANSWER TO A SIMPLE QUESTION LIKE I ASKED HER! WHAT A DUMMY!"

Miss Green suddenly finds herself in a "lose-lose" situation. Her best means of coping would be to laugh it off, offering some relaxed and playful rejoinders like: "That's the way it goes — I didn't take my SMART pills this morning!" Such a reply not only would quickly defuse the seriousness of the moment, but would also allow her to take responsibility for her "memory loss" — as opposed to a popular alternative chosen by many in such situations . . . striking back at the source of the aggravation. Aiming to demean the student as a means of "saving face" consumes a disproportionate amount of energy. Responding to stress with aggression is far more costly in terms of energy spent than is ever gained in return.

Honesty is the best technique for dealing with such situations. It is far better than any other method. Some theorists try to analyze behavior represented in verbal exchanges. This technique is particularly popular in transactional analysis, or "TA," as it is often called. Such systems of analysis are interesting, but can be put in total perspective by considering the concept of honesty. The necessity for having elaborate schemes for understanding the various roles operating in verbal exchanges is greatly diminished when one is simply *honest*. Being honest is simple, elegant, and the best of all possible ways to reduce stress.

Teachers are *not* the only ones in school settings to experience stress. It's hard to determine WHO experiences the most — the students, always judged, always participants in a game with changing rules and no referees; the teachers, pawns on their own invented game boards; the administrators, vulnerable to parents constantly threatening to "buy no more games!"; and the parents and community, relaxed enough until they see that none of the games they've bought their kids are interesting or seem to teach them anything. The kids are always bored.

Extremes certainly, but the stresses are there — in most people some of the time, and in too many people most of the time. For more on STRESS, its characteristics, and different means to check it out and deal with it . . . see the "Personal Harvests" chapter later in this book.

Remember that STRESS doesn't have to be a weed . . . Try this:

the only way to grow is straight fearward

Activities

In each person's life, there are a number of things they *quit* doing . . . sometimes . . . because of stress.

This condition is often called "burn-out." Check your own experience — and focus on what you did after you quit doing what caused the stress.

Is burn-out the appropriate term?
Is burn-out a negative term?

Indicators of Stress . . . Symptoms of Burnout Becoming . . .
- persistent feeling of exhaustion, as in "I'm just so tired . . ."
- never being awake to see Johnny Carson
- always being awake for Johnny Carson, but grading papers instead
- always being hungry
- never being hungry (check both if applicable)
- bubbling feelings of hostility throughout each day
- consistent negative response to statement, "There's nothing I'd rather be doing than this."
- never seeking new ideas, never having time for old ones.

List ten things no one has any right to expect of you. (Example: making lists.)

List ten things you have no right to expect of others.

Now switch lists — and see if they still make sense. Refer to these lists again when you get to Chapter 13.

TAKING ATTENDANCE

(Have you ever wondered who you take attendance from?)

Most schools have generated an efficient, or at least standard, mechanism for getting attendance data to the school office. But collecting the data is often your responsibility. You can approach this task in several ways:

1. Through building a habitual technique for taking attendance. This approach provides for efficient performance of an assigned task. An assigned seating chart at 8:40 each day allows for minimal hassle and quick response to the task.

2. Through generating new and creative attendance-taking strategies. The key here is ingenuity and playfulness. A week of scorecards, for example:

```
Theodore Roosevelt Intramural
        Attendance League
FIRST TRIAL (and sometimes error)
Date of Trial- May 2
Game played on Mr.Barry's Court
Score:      ATTENDERS    27
            ABSENTEES    3
 Scoring for the ABSENTEES:
     Bill Schwartz- on disabled list (flu)
     Sally Burgess- a rumored trade (to
                    Suddville Elementary)
     Tim Billings- Again our lead scorer
                   strikes for freedom

 Scoring for the ATTENDERS:
     George Laslow nearly scored for the
     opposition but rallied to pull a
     simple tardy (thank you Mr.Counselor)
```

3. Through delegating responsibility for attendance taking. This approach can take the monkey off your back. For example: (a) use a rotating attendance monitor (this tends to produce dizziness and headaches, especially if the rotator is late, absent, or forgetful); (b) use the old punch-in routine (this has the same disadvantage as it has in assembly-line industry. Absentees have friends too); (c) use teacher's pet (maybe you'd better do it yourself unless you trust everybody).

ASSUMPTIONS

Much of what we do is based on assumptions we carry with us. This baggage is often untagged, unrecognized, lost in transit, and many times completely empty. What assumptions, for instance, underlie the rules which govern schools, such as:

- Every child between the ages of 6 and 16 (or 18) shall attend school 180 days a year except under unusual circumstances, such as illness, etc.
- Kids have to be on the school grounds during school hours.
- Kids can't be on the school grounds after school hours.
- Kids have to "sign out" to go to the lavatory.
- Kids have to have a pass to go anywhere.
- Kids can go to the playground only at recess and lunchtime.
- All visitors must report to the office.

What about some other common practices:
- District offices have carpets and air conditioning. Classrooms don't.
- Administrators and faculty have reserved parking spaces. Students don't.
- Teachers have a lounge. Kids don't.
- There are separate lavatory facilities for teachers and students.
- Students have to use the pay phone. Faculty doesn't.

There are probably very good reasons for all of these things. The point here is not to debate their worth, but to look at the basis for their existence.

OBJECTIVES or OBJECTIONS

A military officer had an impossible task. He was to train his troops in the skills of archery. They were not at all interested. Each time he would set up the targets and order the troops to aim and fire, the entire area was endangered. No one would stay within a kilometer of these would-be William Tells. The troops' lack of interest in archery caused the situation to go from bad to worse. Yet the officer knew that the general was due to inspect progress that very afternoon. When the time came for inspection, the officer marched his troops to a nearby barn. He pointed each soldier in the direction of the barn and ordered them to fire. He then proceeded to paint targets around each arrow with the point of impact as the bulls-eye. Not only was the general impressed with the accuracy of the archers, but the soldiers, having seen their success, began to take a real interest in archery and were soon accomplished bowmen.

This technique can be used in schools, even if the performance objectives are prepackaged. All that is required is that the teacher conduct class as usual (or as unusual, if preferred) and postpone peeking at the list of objectives until midway (or further) through the year. At that time most students will have already accomplished some or many of the objectives. If the natural history of each student has been chronicled, there is an added bonus. Most students will have accomplished many other objectives, not included in the list.

There is no way out of the trap that performance or behavioral objectives are *external* expectations. Students do not have a voice in their production. Adults decide what they will be.

It is basic to the human psyche that people who do not feel they own the objectives they're trying to achieve do not achieve well. If they actually engage in the act of trying to achieve these foreign objectives, they will also have poor self-images.

Objectives are OK

... if you remember that failure is positive feedback as surely as success is! /

What can a teacher do about this situation?

1. You can try to convince the students that the objectives are worthwhile and that it is in their own interest to "adopt" them. Some teachers are good at this. Most of us are not, especially if we too have had problems accepting someone else's agenda.

2. You can try "mixed mediation" by providing specific and regular times for students to identify their own objectives and work toward achieving them. This can take the sting out of the times when other folks' objectives are primary. Or, you can try to weave a fabric of student and institutional objectives into the total program, again diluting the effect of the "accepted" objectives. (Dilution works both ways, however.)

3. You can ignore the institutional objectives and assume (or hope or not care) that they will be accomplished if the kids are productively involved in what they have decided is important.

Most of all, listen to your intuition. If it tells you that reading's really important, the kids will know it. They'll see you reading in every free moment. They'll ask you what you read and why. If you don't do much reading, your intuition isn't telling you it's important, and you're not exhibiting its importance to kids. If your writing is neat and creative, if your body is in good shape, if you don't smoke, if you spell well, if you like to work out math problems, if bugs and snakes interest you, kids will see it. They'll see when none of this interests you, too. You can't really fool them. Most importantly, don't try to fool yourself.

memory

LESSON PLANS—TRAPS OR RESOURCES

Lesson plans are similar to objectives in that they can establish expectations which provide the context for failure. If your school requires an advance copy of lesson plans, you have an additional constraint. Here are some thoughts regarding planning.

1. Never take lesson plans seriously. If you do, they are traps.

2. Always overplan. This is especially important for inexperienced teachers but useful for "old pro's" too. The obvious advantage to overplanning is that if one technique, strategy, set of materials falls flat, you'll have others in mind. Another purpose for overplanning is that when you've got too much to do, you can't take any of it too seriously. (If you still take it seriously and become frustrated because you can't get all of those neat ideas in, it's time for underplanning or not planning at all.)

3. Plan unplanned times. These times are useful for reflecting on what has been done during the planned times and extending learnings into realms of personal interest to students. Transfer of learning is not automatic, so some time to compare marketplace economics to the school cafeteria, for example, can be productive.

4. Spontaneity and flexibility are more important than "covering the book." Learning which occurs in context beats hell out of abstracting contexts. If policemen are on this week's community helpers agenda and Bill falls off the slide and breaks his arm, it's probably more appropriate to study about doctors, nurses, and lawyers.

5. Herb Kohl suggested that a teacher keep two sets of plans — one for show and one for use. We suggest that however you work it, you write a "lesson planned," i.e., document what really happened. Here's a good place to find your "behavioral outcames."

6. Let the kids write your lesson plans sometimes. It provides them with a better feeling for what you're doing, and it might give you a better idea of how kids perceive you. It could even give you some great lessons.

In schools we study history to live in the future.
We learn that "present" is a gift, but we do that
only on holidays.

HOMEWORK

Students seem uniformly to view homework as a weed — but even that doesn't always hold true. Parents have mixed feelings, but tend for the most part to value homework . . . particularly when their children "get it done." Teachers comprise the most varied group of viewers — almost always finding homework in their gardens, whether planted by their choice or creeping in as a weed by virtue of its tenacity in the nearby community.

We think it depends on the quality. An unfair thing, you say, to judge a weed?! But it can be done.

Those award-winning strains of homework flowers are those the students cherish — activities they learn from and find so gratifying that they take them home to improve and share with the family.

It can be persuasively argued that *any* homework serves some purpose . . . but care should be taken to see that it doesn't kill all the *other* plants in the garden.

153

EVALUEATION

spelling

EVALUWEIGHTING

Evaluation is a philosophical act. It takes place in education because it is a part of the philosophy of our culture. Often teachers do it in response to the prevailing notion that exists that it is an integral part of teaching. If one teaches, we are told, to determine the effectiveness of that teaching we should measure how well the job was done.

As innocent as this sounds, it is surprising that evaluation becomes the largest weed patch in educational experience. It is expensive. It uses up about 40 percent of most teaching time. It is the basis for most of the money that is asked for in the tax base levied against a community. It is the primary element of multimillion-dollar industries (the standardized test services). It is the core of fiscal morality of most educational systems, meaning that "good" education is weighed against "bad" education on the basis of some form of evaluation.

Evaluation is an expression of a culture. In our culture it is basically aggressive. It is a thing "done" to someone. As a result, it creates a great deal of stress. Unlike certain Native American cultures in which evaluation is primarily conversational, our dominant culture makes it judgmental. This results in it being hard on both teachers *and* students. And administrators too.

The basic question concerning evaluation is: CAN HONESTY, COMPASSION, AND GROWTH BE WOVEN INTO AN ACT OF AGGRESSION?

154

EVALUHATING/EVALULOVING

Evaluation is one of those "weeds" you can't get rid of. Administrators view it as a cash crop. It is also something we all do all the time anyway. Our personal evaluations may not be as organized or formal as standardized tests or grading-period quizzes, but they are just as real. There are some things that can be done to make evaluation more palatable and even more useful.

1. Tell students which evaluations are being used for grades and which are not.
2. Spend time discussing diagnostic evaluations with individual students. Discussion includes LISTENING.
3. Try to have several techniques available for everything you want to evaluate: tape recorders for poor writers, butcher paper and paints for those into graphics, clay and wood for model builders. (Yes, answers can be given which are not words.)
4. Collections of what students do are probably the best single tool for recording "progress." If the kids have the choice of what goes in such a collection, it is even more fair. Kids really do know when what they do is good. Even the 'A' students produce stuff they would not like to be identified with. Artists know when something is good enough to sign. Maybe kids should decide whether to sign their papers or not.

I don't give gold stars, but if I did I'd give them for:
  ☆ *faltering starts, for at least they are starts.*
  ☆ *changing minds, for they show that the mind is active.*
  ☆ *bad ideas, for they indicate a willingness to search for good ones.*
  ☆ *unrealistic plans, for without castles in the air we'd not know where to put foundations.*

A list of Statements to Make to Marsha's Parents at Open House

I refuse to say that Marsha is inferior to the rest of the students, for by doing so I unnecessarily demean Marsha and minimize the gains she has made.

I refuse to say that Marsha is "normal" or average, for then I place her in the position where her unique talents are diminished in importance.

I refuse to say that Marsha is superior to other students, because by doing so I have lowered, in your eyes and mine, our opinions of the other students.

Therefore, I will speak of what Marsha has accomplished and will show you what she has done and will share with you my perceptions of her and ask you to do the same.

155

GRADES

Grades are much like homework. Not much liked by most of the kids most of the time. Not much liked by teachers, especially when they have to "explain" them. Not much liked by parents except when they are "good."

Grades and evaluation have a lot in common, but not as much as some might think.

The most useful of grades are those that communicate something to others and — most importantly — in a meaningful and instructive way to the individuals being "graded." THAT'S NOT THE WAY IT IS MOST OF THE TIME!

In case anyone might still be immersed in delusion . . .

Evaluation and its common technique, grading, are among the most explosive concepts in all of education. All kinds of rhetoric exist about how grading is done to "let the students know where they are." People who claim this usually think their grading is objective . . . They defend grading on spelling, adding, subtracting, and multiplying as being objective. In a way, they are right. However, how they *use* those grades determines the next step. Do they compare one child's grades with another's? Do they use a change in the grades or the level of the grades as a basis for getting more federal or state funding?

Grades and evaluation are deeply intermeshed with the values of a culture. What we grade, we value. A child's degree of conformity to what we value often establishes a view of that child's worth.

But some kinds of grading can be more objective than others.

We find it useful to do some sorting of the different kinds of grading. In doing that, we find plenty of weeds and a good number of roses — gorgeous, enhancing plants with a number of irritating thorns if care is not taken in handling them.

Attitude Inventories:

This form of evaluation tries to determine the basic posture of student "attitudes" about things . . . particularly about things that affect school. Typically paper-and-pencil, multiple-choice-filled sheets of statements for which you select the most appropriate response in view of your feelings about the subject; these are frequently used to "get federal funding," get someone a job, or "find an excuse to can" someone else.

The intentions? To find out how people are *feeling* about things that affect them. That's laudable. In our society, however, most often more meaningful and effective ways to get the same information are to talk with and listen carefully to the people involved, over time.

Diagnostic Tools

These can really be tools — but often are used as weapons.

Used most often to determine students' reading, writing, and mathematical ability, they end up putting the students in boxes.

Picture this:

Student takes "special" test. Student isn't told before or after anything *about* the test. Just told he or she is going to take it. Anxiety builds in the student. The test is special — but no one tells the student what is special about it.

The student takes the test. No one says anything afterwards, not even when the results are "in."

Two weeks later the student is transferred to a "special" class. Pick your label . . . it might be "Bluebirds," "eagles," "turtles" or "lizards," it might be "remedial," it might be "canaries," it might be "average," it might be "chocolate chip cookies," it might be "advanced." Whatever the category, it does as much to create the problem as to arrest it.

Diagnostic tools *can* be used humanely; to inform the students, parents, and anyone else concerned about each student's specific skills — not compared to other students so much as to mastery of some specific skill.

Involve the student over time in the process of diagnosis, how it's done, and what it means, and then share with the student the very real indications of mastery of the skill that appear.

Then the process isn't meaningless or onerous — it is a healthy part of each student's interest in personal growth and development.

158

Subject-Matter Exams

These can be such exciting instruments . . . and yet all too often they are used as foreign incendiary devices to set student's concepts of self off in flames.

It is a great gift to study some subject of interest and then measure yourself against (some part of) that mountain of content you tried to explore. If you care about the subject, and your first effort to test how well you remember the paths you took and what you found shows you got lost along the way . . . hope that someone will provide you with the opportunity to explore again, finding markers along the way to help you remember where you've been and where you're going.

Too often, tests are the teacher's invention and are totally unrelated to items of worth and relevance to students (much less what teacher and students "covered" together in class).

If the subject matter really is worth learning, let the students participate along the way in pointing out things to remember; let them test themselves (even using the teacher's invented maps); and if the results aren't sufficient to indicate to either the student or the teacher that the student could find the way again . . . give the student another chance.

Another way is to test the *class* rather than the student. Using three or four different tests with the items printed on little slips of paper, each student can pick out a dozen questions and answer them on the slip. The teacher then scores the responses of the entire class. Another simpler way is to get the students to respond on answer sheets and turn them in with no name on them.

This process yields useful information — no one is comparing one student's map reading to other map readers in the class. What's going on is simply a way of seeing if each student can find the way to get someplace she or he wants to go!

Report Cards

It's hard to see much of anything but weeds when looking at these — at least if they're the kind filled with letter grades denoting some quality of work. They simply are not too useful — except in perpetuating all kinds of mythologies about the kinds of students who are "A" students, "B" students, "F" students, etc. (Number grades like 1, 2, 3, 4, and 5 serving the same purpose are just as troublesome.)

Number grades, such as 80 out of 100, can be instructive . . . if the student and the teacher know exactly what those numbers are based on, they are constant, and each student has continued opportunities to evidence the knowledge necessary to improve mastery of the content.

Lists of skills can be useful . . . with very straightforward indications as to whether students can do them . . . or not. It is often useful and instructive to let students add some skills *they* value to the list, indicating whether or not they can do them. Parents could add some too.

Written evaluations in combination with both of the above — numbered scores against some given subject matter, and indications of mastery of various valued skills — can be highly meaningful. These can provide a chance to record the students' view of that they have learned in the grading period . . . commenting about feelings related to that learning, and including honest appraisals of their effort. But to do this, the teacher risks violating tradition. If you do, get ready for a lot of bewilderment on the part of parents, students, and other teachers. One who chooses to try this form of evaluation must know it works *only* if the others in the chain are covered. Parents have to know what the process is and what it means. So do other teachers.

Teachers should write an evaluation of each of their students too — reporting for posterity the topics covered, sources used, directions taken, attitudes expressed, moments of sorrow, moments of joy.

The PROBLEM with this approach is the difficulty of any teacher's writing a great number of these evaluations. Take the secondary teacher with 160 students. That's a problem.

BUT IT REALLY ISN'T INSURMOUNTABLE!

Evaluations can be recorded on tape — and transcribed by somebody else.

Evaluations can be restricted to subject matter — recording only the teacher's view of what was presented and emphasized using what resources . . . with other measures such as those suggested above (SOME of those suggested above!) to indicate what the students DID with the subject matter.

Do the evaluations in manageable batches rather than all at one time. This allows a freshness to be sustained. Evaluation fatigue is disastrous for both teacher *and* student.

160

Just because you think it can't be done ... doesn't mean it's not worth trying —

But I tried though... I sure as hell did that much.......
McMURPHY — ONE FLEW OVER THE CUCKOO'S NEST

BEING EVALUATED

This "weed" is one which pops up periodically. Many schools have procedures which make teacher evaluation a yearly proposition. The techniques vary, as do the criteria. You might be "measured" on anything from your *loving attitude toward students* to *how many days you were late for work*. Formal evaluation is usually done by administrators, but you're always being evaluated by someone: peers, students, parents, yourself.

Some comments regarding formal evaluation:

1. You have a right to know the criteria. Ask for a list.
2. *Invite* the evaluator to your class. Don't wait for an unexpected appearance.* Do it by memo so it's in writing. And submit a list of things you insist on the evaluators being aware of. You have the right to have a say about the criteria on which you will be judged.
3. Request a conference to discuss the evaluation after you've been observed.
4. Treat the evaluation as a learning experience instead of as a Gestapo technique.

If you do these things, you'll probably get a better rating for initiative and cooperation. You'll also stimulate your administrator to be very conscientious regarding your particular evaluation.

---

* Sometimes it's better not to know. We know one teacher who had only one evaluation conference in four years. The administrator said that his observation had shown only one weak spot. The teacher mentioned that he couldn't recall being observed in those four years. The principal said, "Oh! I listened in over the P.A. system." The shocked teacher asked what the weak spot was. The principal said, "Your room was too noisy."

The trick is to make this whole crazy process of teaching and learning meaningful — particularly to the people it most greatly affects . . . the students.

No matter what system your school employs for dealing with these living things (whether you and they see them as weeds or as flowers) . . . treat them with care, thought, honesty, and humor. Even the most serious things . . . can be taken *too* seriously.

Oops I'm sorry I tore it.

The Remeadial Spellers Tribuet *

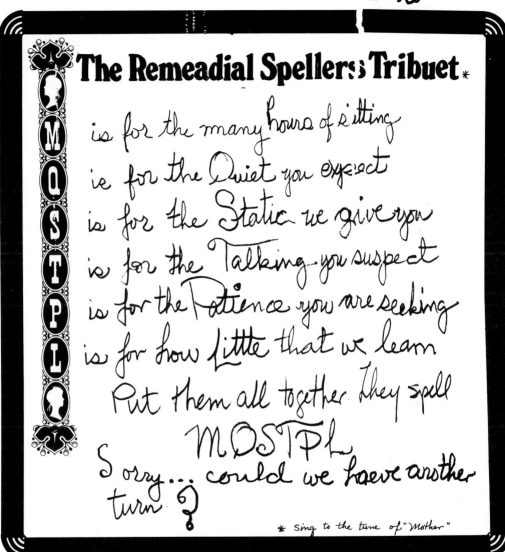

M is for the many hours of sitting

Q ie for the Quiet you expect

S is for the Static we give you

T is for the Talking you suspect

P is for the Patience you are seeking

L is for how Little that we learn

Put them all together they spell

MOSTPL

Sorry... could we have another turn?

* sing to the tune of "Mother"

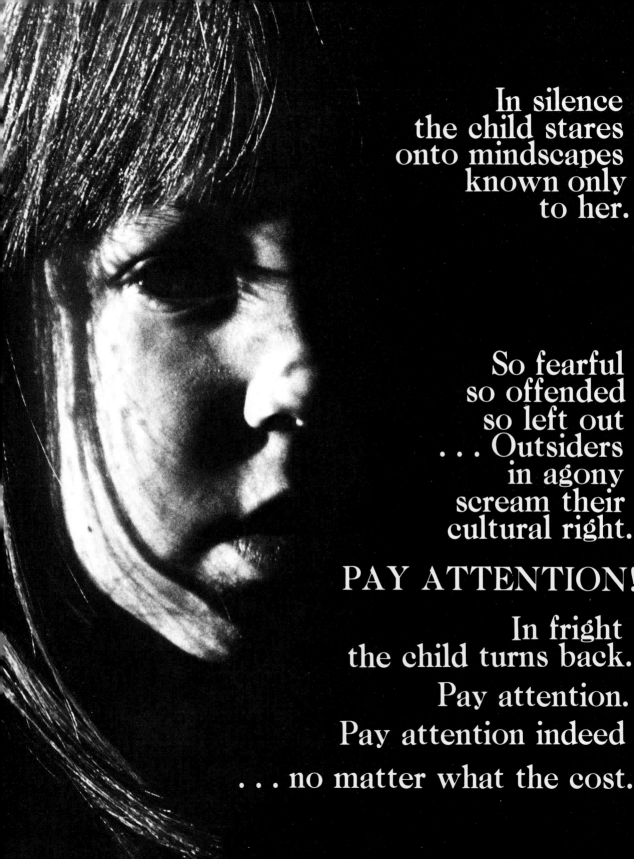

In silence
the child stares
onto mindscapes
known only
to her.

So fearful
so offended
so left out
... Outsiders
in agony
scream their
cultural right.

PAY ATTENTION!

In fright
the child turns back.
Pay attention.
Pay attention indeed
... no matter what the cost.

Gardens of Culture
II

As we have said many times, educational philosophy and psychology apply not only to what you do, but also to how you do it. This means that *what a person knows* and *the way he or she gets exposed to that knowing* are both vital to the process called education. In this section of THE WHOLESCHOOL BOOK, we will focus on the ways that people within our culture become involved in the process of learning. We will look at the ways that people have been allowed to act while engaged in the process of learning. And we will look at the choices you can make as one who creates learning environments . . . choices affecting both *what* and *how* people learn in your presence.

165

Schools are able to provide almost devastatingly accurate portraits of human history. What this means is that they generally exhibit practices and procedures that nearly all other segments of a culture have gone beyond. Only recently have schools in some areas of the United States begun to point the way toward the future. This most certainly doesn't mean that all schools are the same. If they were, there would be little to talk about.

Some of you who read these words have experienced a model of education changed little from medieval times. Others of you have experienced a strong dose of assembly-line schooling in which everything but the view outside the window — if there was one — was packaged and delivered. Others of you may know the "mystery-school" model, where it takes till Thanksgiving to discover who the teacher is. All of those models and others are out there right now — today! In this section we will discover what they mean to teachers and students.

Charles Reich, in a controversial book called *The Greening of America*, labeled three distinct philosophical stages of American cultural consciousness: Consciousness I, Consciousness II, and Consciousness III. Critics of Reich's work are numerous. Some say his stages are vague and not documented well. Others say he stopped too soon. We use his models here because they are useful . . . not because they are true.

Consciousness I was the era of the Puritan ethic.
Consciousness II is the era of the technocratic ethic.
Consciousness III is the era of the emergence of the intrinsic ethic.

In each stage of consciousness, the culture created a characteristic mode for the conduct of education that embodied the basic vision the culture had of itself.

IT'S A NO-NO
TO KNOW NO
NEW KNOWS

DIDACTIC MODE

The didactic mode is found in places where there is high agreement concerning what students should *know*. The roots of what we call the didactic mode as used in the United States lie in the Puritan ethic. CONTENT — the stuff that is to be learned — is clearly identified, and it is comprised of the significant facts and skills universally agreed to be possessed by the educated person. History, literature, and civics are the important disciplines. Reading, writing, and arithmetic are the important skills. These were the disciplines and skills valued in our emerging nation.

Schools were definitely instruments of the church at the outset. Harvard College was founded to train the clergy in this new world. The schools the children attended were laced with religious experience. Inherent in this vision of school was the supremacy of content. Content was king. There was little or no question about *what* was to be known. In terms of the way it was to be learned, there was likewise little question. The act of learning required moral discipline to match the authority of the academic disciplines being taught. Students were required to be respectful and obedient as they were taught what was TRUE knowledge. As a result, the procedures for teaching were highly structured, as was the curricular content. The teacher was the ultimate authority. Students spoke when spoken to, wrote when told to, and never questioned unless given permission.

This approach to education was hugely efficient. That which was taught was expected to be that which was learned. Modification of facts and skills was neither expected nor tolerated. Evaluation was simple. Whatever the teacher gave to the students was that which was to be returned . . . unaltered, unchanged, and perfect. The teacher . . . an authoritative source. And the student . . . a willing and respectful receptacle.

The culturally approved of vision for content was that it was unchangeable. In many ways, this approach to content was the result of blending the view of the authority of religion with the authority of knowledge. This led to a kind of educational contradiction, because the very presence of this "new world" was a testimonial to revolution — to change. The spoken ethic was to maintain the status quo and keep things the same. At the same time, everyone was immersed in a milieu of change prevailing everywhere and all around them.

168

NOTE: Don't mistake telling something or lecturing to someone as necessarily being didactic in the mold of true believer's motivation. You may just be informing that person of your beliefs. Or using a highly efficient technique for transmitting information. You are engaging in Puritan ethic-didactic tactics if you think that what you believe is absolutely TRUE, and that anyone listening (and they all *should* be listening!) is wrong or stupid if they don't believe you!

The didactic mode is the classic form of what we call a *delivery* approach to education. Delivery approaches to education take the form of modes in which *the content and the process of learning are essentially delivered to the students*.

Teaching strategies characteristic of the didactic delivery mode are lectures by the teacher and oral recitations, drill and review, and rote memory work by the student.

PROCESS MODE

With the dawning of the assembly line in the United States, a new kind of approach to teaching emerged. Mass production and organized teamwork became an ethical vision that was far more compatible with the growing nation than was the earlier idea that nothing could change. The new nation, with its richness in resources and energy, was awesomely more seductive than tradition had been. Development of industry, commerce, and exploitation of natural resources became the primary focus of the new immigrants. It was not long before people spent most of their time and energy on growth rather than on maintaining the status quo.

Only about four generations of post-Pilgrim Americans were needed to shift the life-styles of the people from a dominantly agricultural country rich in Old World tradition to a new land of burgeoning commerce and industry. With industry, the new ethic of production, teamwork, and competition was created out of the older vision of escape from oppression. To be godly now was to grow. To grow, the individual families had to organize their work to be more efficient than it had been. But to grow was also to compete. In less than two more generations, the nation went from an ethic of being a collection of oppressed individuals who had been punished for their beliefs and had to be reminded of it, to a new ethic of competitive striving for growth. This meant that most gave up the idea that truth was unchangeable. Curriculum kept its traditional categories, but soon began to reflect the new ethic.

Political competition, religious competition, and industrial competition became such dominant forces that eventually competitive entertainment was invented. Team sports were born. Baseball, basketball, and soccer all emerged in nearly present form. Comparable forms of school and education were to follow. The *way* things were done became more important than *what* was done. True, content was not abandoned, but it did take second place to learning to play the game. Growth was identified in terms of an external, material universe. How much control could one gain over it? Success and status could be obvious to others.

Society was thus reveling in the success of the technocracy during the late 1950s. On the whole, however, modes of education had not changed too drastically from the traditional didactic mode just described. But as we know, history can change the lives of human beings. Schools were soon to change to more accurately reflect the changes in the rest of society, but they got a large boost with the rocketing success of the Soviet Sputnik in 1957. The United states's horror was real in the face of this obvious threat to competitive excellence. If the Russians could succeed in doing something we had not yet been able to do, there must be *something* wrong with our schools. With millions of dollars of federal money as one real impetus, attention was turned to improving the quality of education in American public schools. Since — in the face of rapid technological advances — content was always changing, attention was focused on strategies for teaching and learning. If the *what* students learn is going to keep changing, let's put more attention on the *ways* students learn.

As might be expected, a sort of overreaction took place. Many of the characteristic strategies of the didactic mode were blanketly rejected, largely because of the psychological onus they carried with them — not because of their ineffectiveness as teaching strategies.

We call the kind of approach to educational practice which emerged . . . the process mode. You may find many examples of the curriculum materials representative of this mode in what we and others fondly refer to as the alphabet-soup curricula of the 1960s and 1970s.

But even though these materials and others of this period were characterized by a new emphasis on involving the student in the process of learning, for the most part the determination of the content and the way the content would be learned were still determined by someone other than the student. Even when using the "inquiry method" (a process mode we have been heard to call glibly the "inquisition method") — where students are to discover for themselves the routes to obtaining the desired knowledge — the steps to be taken by the students in their process of discovery were determined largely by the scholars (who verified the content), the curriculum developers (who put the package together), and the teachers (who made it available to the students).

So the process mode is another *delivery* mode. Characteristic teaching strategies involve teacher and student discussion, usually but not always directed by the teacher; "hands-on" laboratory experiences to simulate the process of scientific discovery; and use of varied media to appeal to differing styles of learning.

INTRINSIC MODE

A predictable outcome of a cultural dominance by authority and competition is a kind of backlash move toward the assertion of individual integrity. Many argue that this existed in the early days of the colonies and was lost as the technocratic ethic grew. Whether true or not doesn't matter, as recent years have witnessed a definite surge toward such individual expression. The dominant oppressive routines of prejudice in our culture are being severely questioned. Racism, sexism, adultism, and ageism are becoming issues for far greater numbers of people, as in some way all are victims. Each individual has fewer freedoms because these prejudices against some exist.

Individuals are also becoming vividly agitated about the constant ecology of competition that prevails. Serious questions are being asked concerning the validity of competition as a condition for growth.

Growth in and of itself is becoming an issue of concern. The concepts of cooperation and culture in equilibrium are being popularized in many areas. The public media have probably played a far more important role in this emergence than have the schools. However, in the last decade or so the effect of all this has begun to make a difference in the schools.

With the access mode to teaching engaged, competition loses its unquestioned cultural status. Each person chooses personal life standards and becomes more individualized. What this means is that when individuals choose not to follow the rules, they have not only a new ball game, but also one that defies external control. In curriculum, it forces the concern for education to become aimed at the individual rather than wholly at either the content (what is taught) or the process (the way it is learned). Instead, it requires both of these to be of concern at once. But each individual gets to set the priorities.

With a description like that, it sounds as though utter disaster would be the result. In some cases, that *has* been the result — or nearly. We have seen lots of excesses in the name of open and alternative education, but suspect that many of these were necessary as a part of a natural cycle of change.

We think it is possible for the access mode as an approach to education to become a reality in the public schools of the United States. It is already flourishing quietly in a remarkable number of classrooms in widely varying geographic regions of the country. This mode is an *access* approach to education. In such an approach, students are legitimate decision makers. They can determine what content they will study and what means they will take in the process of study. But they will not make such decisions in a vacuum. They will do so in partnership with a skilled and sensitive teacher . . . one who is flexible, competent, and (you remember!) has a sense of humor. Such a teacher must know enough about subject matter to be interesting — and to know that he or she doesn't know everything. And enough about process to know there are many ways to learn.

172

THE CONTENT EQUALS THE PROCESS
AND THE PLACE IS EVERYWHERE !

Education in such settings is orchestrated toward synergy. Competence in content is not overlooked, and competition is not denied. It is just that neither of these becomes a necessary and sufficient condition to explain all the acts of teaching and learning. In this mode, all of the preceding teaching strategies used in the didactic and process modes can be viable and appropriate at certain times and in certain cases. Tradition is cherished and no content or approach is automatically omitted. But in every case, in this mode of instruction, all the possibilities for content and process are made available. Yet they are called into play by each student as each chooses to extend his or her experience and knowledge. This basic condition stands in contrast to the choice being made wholly by someone other than the student.

"... so to teach in to "deny the richness deny the worth of it is an affirmation is in becoming a the students ... and facilitate their decisions about _what_

the intrinsic is not
of authority ... not to
process ... But rather
of both. The uniqueness
human partner of
to enrich and
role in making
and how they can
learn !

Write assignments for each of the modes related to the following concepts:
- the democratic process
- cultural pluralism
- the energy crisis
- the structure of poetry
- gravity
- levity
- Archimedes Principal (he *did* leave teaching)
- scarcity in economics
- evolution
-
-
-
-

Didactic

Process

Intrinsic

Synergic Settings

love, friendship, creativity, learning to
walk, learning to speak, learning to
dance, skiing, cooking by taste, playing
music by ear, raising children, intuition,
insight, outsight, writing poetry,
remembering smells, inventing, singing,
love making, being surprised, being
emotional, reaching the top of a
mountain no one saw you climb, seeing
the Grand Canyon, watching sunrise or
sunset over the sea, realizing that all
humans are *one* and that they are
different, learning anything . . .

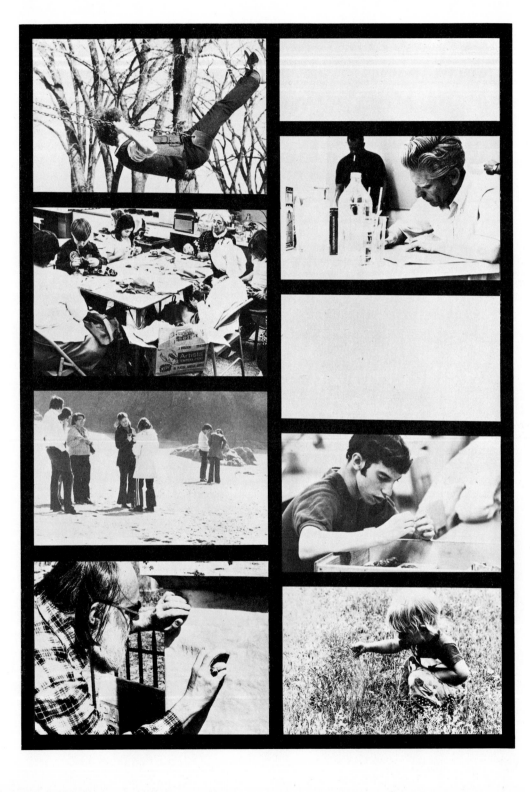

There is so much confusion about how one should teach and what one should teach that one commonly forgets about learning. Learning is the natural-born, innate profession built into all our genes. And yet our culture believes it must train (and certify) teachers. Our environment guarantees that learning will take place. The issue in this section has been to examine the consequences of three distinct approaches to teaching and learning.

There is no question that the setting one creates for another to experience will affect the kind of learning that takes place. The way we have put this book together and the words and images we have chosen have affected the kind of learning you have experienced in reading it. We know our choices have affected you, but only you know *how*. Some of you like weird books, and this one may seem conservative to you. Others may like books that aren't all screwed up with pictures, oversized letters, miniposters, and planning that require you to turn pages sideways and upside down. In any case, all of you have learned something from our choices. Some found little new; others a lot. Some found this book useful for pressing flowers.

So too do the various modes of instruction affect learning. None of these is the last word. As much as anything, each represents a stage in the educational evolution of a culture. The one thing to remember is that *any* content can be didactic. *Any* process can be didactic. Thus even what we have described as the access mode can be as limiting and competitive as those dealt with in earlier periods of this country's history — if dealt with as being THE TRUTH.

12
Seeds and Germination

Plants have a simplicity
that transforms
our ways of knowing.

They cannot
be commanded to grow.

They can be injured
—and still continue to grow.

They do not grow
where they cannot
unless tended to.

If there is sun, soil and water
. . . plants not only grow
. . . but also renew themselves
as seasons pass.

Schoolwork when done badly is quickly forgotten or remembered with distaste years later when the learner is reminded. When done well it provides skills and knowledge that persist throughout life. This section of THE WHOLE SCHOOL BOOK is aimed at providing you with an array of activities consistent with the ACCESS mode described in earlier chapters of this book. These are activities assigned to transform any concept into a more holistic learning experience for students. These are activities designed to nurture ways of knowing that *can* be celebrated by students throughout their lives.

The activities and strategies we have included are not commonly found in standard sources. Most instructional materials in use in public schools today have been created consistent with rational styles of knowing. They tend to be based on a view of intellectual maturation as represented by Piaget and the cognitive psychologists. Logic and sequence provide the organizational framework for these instructional materials. Teaching strategies included in those materials tend to come in the form of what we have described as DELIVERY modes and rely heavily on reading, writing, computation, and skills of logic and thinking.

Since virtually all instructional materials presently in use in public schools have been designed in this fashion — and since among those materials many excellent activities and strategies can be found — we will provide you here with examples of the kinds of activities and strategies you can enjoy using with students and that speak to what we call metaphoric ways of knowing. We will provide you here with those activities and strategies you *can't* find in most other sources. By combining the kinds of activities and strategies we present here with those activities and strategies you can find in other sources, you will be able to create instructional settings in which holistic and what we call synergic learning can take place.

The real advantage to metaphoric knowing is that it lasts longer.

In the pages that follow, the activities and strategies we have included are divided into several major headings. The first four headings — Symbolic:Visual, Synergic-Comparative, Integrative, and Inventive — are all modes of knowing we associate with what we call metaphoric mind function. A detailed explanation, including their theoretical base, can be found in the book THE METAPHORIC MIND (Addison-Wesley, 1976). Rational and metaphoric kinds of knowings can be nurtured by different kinds of instructional strategies. Rational strategies are basically linear, whereas metaphoric strategies are multidimensional.

The definitions we offer here are primarily for those who require a basis for writing objectives and evaluation instruments. If those aren't necessary for you, we offer these constructs because we think they are interesting and might be useful. It is not, however, necessary to understand them in order to create interesting and useful learning activities for students.

THE SYMBOLIC METAPHORIC MODE

Definition: The symbolic metaphoric mode is expressed whenever concepts, experiences, processes, or ideas are expressed in either abstract or visual form.

THE SYNERGIC COMPARATIVE MODE

Definition: The synergic-comparative mode involves the blending of two or more concepts, ideas, and processes so as to transform their original meaning into a more universal context.

THE INTEGRATIVE MODE

Definition: The integrative mode exists when the entire body of the learner is involved in the exploration of concepts, ideas, and processes.

THE INVENTIVE MODE

Definition: The inventive mode exists whenever the learner creates a level of understanding of a concept, idea, or process new to themselves personally or new to the culture in which they live.

natural capacity | **school experience**

Columns (both sides): SYMBOLIC (Abstract, Visual), SYNERGIC COMPARATIVE, INTEGRATIVE, INVENTIVE

Rows: FORMAL OPERATIONAL, CONCRETE OPERATIONAL, PRE-OPERATIONAL, SENSORY MOTOR

FIGURE ONE

IMPLICATIONS OF THE METAPHORIC MODES

Central to the formulation of the metaphoric modes was the issue of how they could fit into schools as they exist. A second issue was our concern about how the metaphoric modes relate to the rational developmental levels of Piaget.

This led us to the next step. We examined existing curriculum materials, standardized tests, and the prevailing psychological vision (cognitive and behavioristic) and tried to determine at which levels of schooling the metaphoric modes were systematically excluded. The results are shown in Figure One. It was clear to us that the *capacity* to perform all the metaphoric modes is uniform throughout the rational stages of development. However, it was also clear that in terms of school experience there is a diminishing utilization of all the metaphoric modes except symbolic abstract as one goes up through the cognitive stages.

185

**In the presence of ambiguity
A child must decide.**

**In the presence of specificity
A child must perform.**

**If I value decision-making
If I value specific skills**

Then I must celebrate both.

SYMBOLIC VISUAL MODE

Visual representations of concepts call a different part of the brain into action than do abstract, logical symbols such as words and numbers. By representing concepts visually, one *ensures a wider and more complete* mental experience than by use of verbal symbols alone. Besides that, things are easier to remember when explored this way!

Paint a portrait of:
- gravity
- democracy
- freedom
- $F = ma$
- the expanding universe
- a fragile edge
- an inside-out tepee
- etc.

Make picture flash cards (use no words!) to represent:
- each of the Departments of the U.S. President's Cabinet, like Treasury, Interior, etc.
- parts of an ecosystem
- parts of speech
- etc.

Make a symbol with color and shape for:
- peace
- war
- divorce
- marriage
- birth
- death
- etc.

Find materials around your house out of anything you think might work... like soggy coffee grounds, leftover breakfast jam, fireplace ashes, newspapers, etc. Use these to create an image of:
- life 100 years ago
- a perfect scene in nature
- a necessary invention
- etc.

Create a map of:
- scary places
- old people in the city
- places where fires start
- cold in a room
- groundsquirrel holes
- etc.

GUIDED IMAGERY

Imagery is almost totally a Learning Poet function. With this strategy we invite its full participation. The idea is simple. We just structure a daydream. It can be about anything, to anywhere, with anyone, or alone. It can be long, short, related to something you're studying or not. We use *words* to get into the process — but once there, images take over!

Tips: Relaxed positions are helpful. (Carpets for lying on are ideal. A Magic Carpet time for primary school kids?) As few distractions as possible will make the first few experiences easier. A soothing but audible voice is best. For those who can't get themselves to participate, an alternative quiet activity will cut down on embarrassed giggles. Leave lots of "empty" space both in terms of specific content and time to visualize. If you've got an agenda, don't expect everybody will meet it. There are lots of interesting side roads on any trip.

Here's an example. (Read it, then close your eyes and do it.)

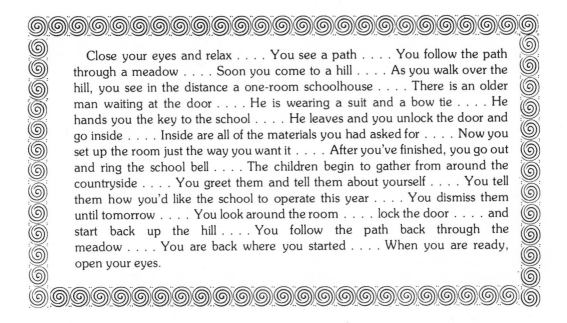

Close your eyes and relax . . . . You see a path . . . . You follow the path through a meadow . . . . Soon you come to a hill . . . . As you walk over the hill, you see in the distance a one-room schoolhouse . . . . There is an older man waiting at the door . . . . He is wearing a suit and a bow tie . . . . He hands you the key to the school . . . . He leaves and you unlock the door and go inside . . . . Inside are all of the materials you had asked for . . . . Now you set up the room just the way you want it . . . . After you've finished, you go out and ring the school bell . . . . The children begin to gather from around the countryside . . . . You greet them and tell them about yourself . . . . You tell them how you'd like the school to operate this year . . . . You dismiss them until tomorrow . . . . You look around the room . . . . lock the door . . . . and start back up the hill . . . . You follow the path back through the meadow . . . . You are back where you started . . . . When you are ready, open your eyes.

Sometimes, not always, the trip is debriefed. This can be private or, if there are volunteers, public.

What did you see on your walk? Were there things that surprised you? Colors? Sounds? Smells? How did you feel when you saw the school? How did you feel when you were given the key? What was the room like? What materials were there? How did you set up the room? Were the children happy? Were you? What did you tell them? Did any of them react or respond? Did you want to leave? Do you want to go back?

There are many variations of the imagery strategy. Small groups of students can lead themselves through a trip, each contributing to the "directions" as they wish. "Canned" cassetted trips can be placed at a "Cheap Field Trip" center with a tape player and earphones. Kids can take each other through the experience. Aggression between two students can be experienced and worked through by having them lead each other through a series of "Yeah, and when you did that to me, I'd. . ." episodes. (Hopefully to end with a "Yeah, and then we decided to stop and . . ." incident.)

What can you use guided imagery for? Here are a few things:
- Building an experience base for inquiry, discussion, group work, etc.
- Creative writing (It's just reporting if you use imagery.)
- Building models (What did the three-dimensional homonym machine look like?)
- Building self-image
- Individualization through group process (All the trips are different)
- Exploring and stretching concepts
- Solving and clarifying problems
- Interpersonal relations
- Exploring history and the future
- Exploring other lands and worlds
- Relaxation
- Raising test scores (Yes, indeed! Do it just before the test.)
- A source of metaphors for Metaphor

SYNERGIC COMPARATIVE MODE

Synergic systems operate by putting concepts and experiences together. The process transforms once separate experiences into a new, richer essence. It is the way yellow and blue blend to make green . . . and soil, water, and sunshine transform a seed into a tree.

All of the following belong together. Find out how!

- dogs, violets, clock parts, voting, and metamorphic rocks
- fish, airplanes, wine bottles, and the second hand on a clock
- paychecks, cottage cheese, acute angles, and chalkboards
- etc.

Inside-out vision forces one to discover the second way anything appears. What is an inside-out:

- pole (a spot, a dot, a pillar, a tube, etc.)
- ocean
- wheel
- war
- election
- savings account
- etc.

Create a new recipe out of well-known ingredients.

FIND NEW WAYS THE FOLLOWING ARE RELATED:

- apples and oranges
- birds and bees
- galaxies and trees
- Republicans and Democrats
- etc.

Combine the Bill of Rights and the instructions for what to do during a fire so a new document emerges. Do what the document says.

INTEGRATIVE MODE

Movement in learning is a very touchy issue. In times past it was restricted to *zero* (sit still and learn!). Now, however, remedial reading is being successfully taught on trampolines, students are dancing the Bill of Rights, and they are pantomiming Newton's laws of motion. These activities all involve the silent use of one's body in the exploration of knowledge. The rewards are infinite . . . for any age learner. For hundreds more examples, see "Movement" from ESSENCE II (Addison-Wesley, 1975).

FULL BODY USE - INDIVIDUAL

Move with your full body in a way that expresses the following:
- succession in nature
- freedom
- Boyle's laws of gases
- etc.

Using any prop *and* your body, express:
- agribusiness
- seed germination
- culture
- etc.

Put your body in a position that represents something you want to know more about. Hold that position for 3 full minutes.

FULL BODY USE - GROUP

With a group, move as the following:
- the water cycle
- erosion and weathering
- the democratic process
- the end of violence
- an era that never was
- transcending ego
- a garden in springtime
- the balance of nature
- tides and the moon
- the simultaneous story lines of any novel
- etc.

Using both hands, show five different ways to mime the following concepts:
- gravity
- love
- addition
- humor
- etc.

As you READ STORIES, HAVE YOUR BODY ASSUME THE POSTURE OF THE CHARACTER YOU ARE READING ABOUT.

Do a hand and head dance to show:
- what you are reading
- a science activity
- what the teacher just said
- the essence of a film you just saw
- etc.

DIRECTOR: THIS IS THE SCENARIO. A CHEMIST IS DOING AN EXPERIMENT. THE FIRST PART OF THE EXPERIMENT INVOLVES PAIRING TWO O's. THE SECOND PART CONSISTS OF TWO PAIRINGS. BOTH PAIRS ARE TO CONSIST OF TWO H's. FINALLY, THE PAIRS ARE TO BE COMBINED APPROPRIATELY. ALL LABORATORY PRECAUTIONS ARE TO BE FOLLOWED, AND THE O's AND H's ARE TO CONSIDER THEMSELVES "FREE AGENTS" UNLESS THE CHEMIST PLACES THEM IN THE LINEUP. THE LINEUP IS CONSIDERED THE LABORATORY SHELF. WHEN I SAY "ACTION" YOU WILL BEGIN. "ACTION!"

(*The ensuing action involved one of the volunteers immediately assuming the role of chemist. She pulled two volunteers from the lineup. They immediately began to move quickly and randomly about the room, frustrating her efforts to get them to pair. She caught them, one at a time, and returned them to the lineup. She then went into the audience and sequestered several volunteers (?) and placed them in a circle. She then took the two volunteers, one at a time, from the lineup and deposited each into the "bottle" she had formed with the audience members. These O's eventually paired with the appropriate sound, and the chemist placed the pair back on the shelf. She then repeated the action with the four H's, leaving them in the bottle. When she "poured" the O pair into the bottle, the pairs united with a spontaneous "BOOOOOOM" and pushed the "bottle" walls in all directions.*)

Audience and director provide applause.

INVENTIVE MODE

Inventive modes are the ones least understood and nurtured in the public schools of the United States. And they are the closest to the source of creativity. One reason is simple. Schools do not differentiate between private, personal invention and public, cultural invention. We celebrate both . . . and think schools can learn to. Each time each student thinks "new," the objective of any inventive mode activity has been met. If students think new in terms of cultural experience, so much the better. But that is not necessary. Maturity in creativity depends on getting a good personal start. Personal inventiveness is typified by the Learning Poet. Public inventiveness is typified by the Learning Censor.

WHOLESCHOOL ACTIVITIES

The following activities and strategies overlap the metaphoric and rational modes. They all nurture synergic learning environments.

RANDOMIZE . . . INSIDEOUT ORDER

Orderliness and structure are the lifeblood of the rational mind. Randomness and nonorder are the lifeblood of metaphoric throught. As a result, in school settings which emphasize rational instruction, students seldom get the chance to *invent* order. Metaphoric thought is what first recognizes patterns to random experience and prepares the experience for action by the rational mind. The following activities focus on those steps of recognition and preparation. Sometimes we take existing order and repattern it. Other times we start from random input.

Anything can be randomized. Just keep in mind that the process of taking order out of an idea is almost the same as creating the order. This gives the student an instant replay, in reverse, about how certain kinds of thinking take place. Again, we are not arguing against rational thought or orderliness; rather, we are arguing for those mindfunctions that *create* order.

Take a walk and note one different object or event every ten steps. Weave linkages and meaning for any ten things you experience in this manner.

Cut up an old copy of a dictionary. (You can do this at a print shop on their trimming press.) Cut it lengthwise between the columns and in three places across each page. Dump all the pieces in a box. Choose any five pieces and use the words on them as a basis for writing a short story.

Tear any ten pages out of a picture magazine (advertisements are fine) and put them together in a sequence that makes sense.

Pick the first three digits of any ten phone numbers in the phone book. Starting with the first set of three, add or subtract the appropriate number to get the second set of three. Repeat with the third and continue until the process results in the last number as the answer to the whole problem. Here's how:

$$\boxed{435} - 0971$$
$$872 - 9421$$
$$631 - 0003$$

$$\boxed{435}$$
$$+ 437$$
$$= \boxed{872}$$
$$- 241$$
$$= \boxed{631}$$

Write any paragraph in five-word columns instead of lines. It works like this: If this is the original statement...

The trees are all blooming at this time of the year. I feel as new as they must.

Then re-order it like this:

The	at	year	as
trees	this	I	they
are	time	feel	must
all	of	as	
blooming	the	new	

After this, add new words in the gaps so that new sentences are created horizontally. It would be like this for the first line:

$\boxed{\text{The}}$ newness $\boxed{\text{at}}$ this time of $\boxed{\text{year}}$ is $\boxed{\text{as}}$ though winter never existed.

TEACHING

fun | bureaucracy | elephants | fragrances | fantasy rivers
boring | administrators | mushrooms | trees | fantasy floats
difficult | kids | clouds | moss | dammed rivers
rewarding | hassles | Rain | sensitivity | Buoyant minstrels
fresh | low pay | drain | | Mellow Bubbles
warming | | clogged | sensor feels | Bubble Raters
exhilarating | Pumpkins | dammed | censor feeling | Bubble Traders
Peace-giving | mush | minstrels | administrate | Dandelion Waters
challenging | dandelions | wastrels | administrape | Dandy Mystics
planning | mystics | fisherpeople | administrap | Mellow trees
reports | reservoirs | Bogs | trapdoor | Mush knees
| Rivers | Piglets | cloud trains |
| mirages | Stars | Rainbrooks |

METAPHOR: A WINDWILLOW WORD WIND

We use the term "metaphor" to describe any nonliteral representation of something (of anything!) Thus a waste basket is a metaphor. For what? For anything you want it to be — except a waste basket. So is a drawing or a juxtaposition of words or a pun or a clay figure.

We also use metaphor to describe a process. Here's how it goes: (1) Collect as many metaphors as you can for whatever topic or concept you want to explore; (2) do something with the metaphors.

An easy way to collect metaphors is on a *very* large sheet of butcher paper. You can act as recorder while folks shout them out; you can let someone else be recorder and get into the act; you can limit the metaphors to particular categories: biological, puns only, words that don't exist, far-out connections, actual visual images; you can have people file up to the butcher paper and write (or draw!) their own . . . .

What do you do with them? Write a poem or paragraph, using only the words on the butcher paper. Pick several metaphors that you wonder about and find out about them through guided imagery (*see* Guided Imagery p. 188) . Paint a picture of a nonsense metaphor you like. Metaphor a metaphor that seems to say something. Dramatize several metaphors through body movement activities. Write a story or play, using metaphors.

Here's one metaphor sheet and a product from it. (The double lines indicate that the recorder changed the rules. The first rule was that there were no rules. The second rule asked for silly metaphors. The third asked for new words, ones that don't exist.)

Cloud Puffs   Learnessence   Teacher tickles   Affect-shuns
Cloud Puff Pie   Learnaches   Kidgrins   Sensilive   Ahead to Basics
Celeb-Rate   Treasure makers   Puddle pleasers   Senses jive   Basic Feelings
Sell-A-Rate   Measure takers   Drop stars   Mellow Rainbow   Basic thoughts
Sell-Abrasion   Joyvibes   Measure makers   Nature's Rainshine   Mesmertears
Trip-ditch   Kissbooks   Kiss Me Quicks   Content tingle   Basic Potential
Rain-a-seance   Miss tooks   Quick No Pain   Content bungle   Smile Stretchers
Tree-Birth   Flagbogs   Homework Drain   Content to bungle
Magic Mirth   Expect-treasures   Calamity Zoo   Silly seasons   Head Stretchers
Mirthaholics   Feather testers   Fuzzy Giggles   People for all seasons
Ticklecolic   Shelf signs   Cogni Giggles   Seasons Pass At
Sensortime   Clean Grins   Read sounds

Teaching is a tender tension between sensorfeels and censor feeling. Mesmertears flood rainrivers of basic feeling, letting sensortime sell-a-rate basic potential. Learnessences are lost to learnaches, treasure makers succumb to measuretakers, and buoyant minstrels drown. But dandymystics make mellow bubbles with visions of magic mirth afloat. Mindstretches tickle head stretchers. Tree birth takes place in hearty soil.

For what can you use a metaphor process? Here are a few things:

- to generate a plan for a unit of study, independent study, group work, a year's work
- to generate assignments for any of the above or for anything else. (Try it with the example. Make up an assignment called "KissBooks.")
- for generating or clarifying problems or concepts.
- to explore attitudes and perceptions. (If you're ready for it, try metaphoring your name with your class.)
- for building visual images or models
- for problem solving
- to explore a concept
- as an instant dictionary. (Beginning writers can write stories, using the words on the butcher paper, and they don't have to chase you around the room to see how to spell.)
- for any subject area
- at teachers' meetings
- with the community
- just for fun

Some comments: Evaluation of metaphors will usually stop them. Don't evaluate. If you're recorder, try not to contribute too much. It can be helpful, once in a while, to write things more than one way, e.g., nation [Nay Shun]; airplane Heir Plain . Participation of the less vocal can be encouraged by nonvocal recording techniques. For heaven's sake, don't take it seriously.

JUNK CENTERS: POSITIVE USES OF THE THROWAWAY SOCIETY

Teaching materials don't have to be expensive. One of our favorite activities in these days of tight and nonexistent budgets for instructional materials is this: Have your students go home and ask their parent(s) to help them gather together a bag full of "usable and interesting junk." With parental permission, the junk should be brought to school (to stay or be recycled in some way). We know of one teacher who literally had all her students dump (gently!) the contents of their bags out onto the floor in the center of the classroom. Then the students spent hours busily and constructively putting everything away! That is, they created systems for inventorying and shelving all the contents of those bags. Once that was done, the *students* knew where everything was, could find whatever they needed whenever they needed it, and everyone benefited by bringing this no-cost resource to the classroom for instructional purposes.

BRICOLEUR . . . .MAKING DO

The *bricoleur* (a French word) is a person who is a solution creator. Shouldn't we say problem solver? No . . . a solution creator is far more competent than a problem solver. This is because a solution creator looks at the world and sees it as a huge universe of solutions rather than as a bewildering array of problems. In everyday terms, a bricoleur not only links up solutions to places where they fit, but also adores inventing the tools necessary to make these linkages. The following activities are ways to broaden one's perceptions of tools and solutions.

Using ten pieces of spaghetti (uncooked) and 25 cm (10 inches) of masking tape, make the tallest tower you can.

Make a boat out of an old book. Float it for 12 hours.

FIND A DOZEN NEW USES FOR ANYTHING.

Make a platform, out of newspapers, that would support your own weight.

Using anything you find in the classroom (except cloth and the first-aid kit), make an emergency bandage for a cut on your hand.

Find the highest number of uses for a potato that does not include eating it.

GO OUTSIDE AND . . .

This little phrase has begun some of the most exciting learning experiences that any of us has experienced. These are the first three words on hundreds of assignments we created for the federally funded transdisciplinary materials called ESSENCE I and ESSENCE II (Addison-Wesley, 1975). (Not all the ESSENCE cards say "Go outside," but enough do, so you get the idea. Sometimes we just mean go outside your everyday perceptions of the world!)

Our reasons were simple. Nature, the community, the out-of-doors are all richer sources of experience than are classrooms. This doesn't deny that classrooms can be rich — but rather emphasizes that the outside world is available . . . and even more rich. It *is* the raw material from which schoolwork is drawn.

Here are a few of the ESSENCE assignments to illustrate:

P THE IDEA THAT EACH PERSON ACTUALLY DECIDES WHETHER OR NOT HE WILL FEEL ANGER, LOVE, ETC. THIS INTERNALIZES THE RESPONSIBILITY. YOU'RE ONLY AS STRONG AS

the action: _____
Make a list of the stupidest things that happen to you in school and a list of the stupidest things you do in school.

Set up a plan to change both. Carry out your plan.

more: _____
• Repeat, using the community, the state, the nation.
• What makes something stu...
• What makes it sma...
• Does it reall...

HE IDEA THAT EACH PERSON ACTUALLY DECIDES WHETHER OR NOT HE WILL FEEL ANGER, LOVE, ETC. THIS INTERNALIZES THE RESPONSIBILITY. KEE

the action: _____
Predict the things that will happen during the day to make you uptight. Keep a record of how good your predictions were. Change the things that happened that you didn't like.

more: _____
•
•

YOU ALLOW YOURSELF TO BE.

Habits

INVENTION BOX

ES ARE OFTEN A

communicate

the action:

In one minute you will become some animal or flower or color or something else . . . Choose what it will and express how it makes you feel any way you choose.

. . . TO ACCEPT. A VERY HIGH TRUST ENVIRONMENT IS NECESSARY FOR PEOPLE TO EXPRESS T. . .

more:
- Find out what happens to you when the system switches off.
- How does each person control the environment?
- What (who) controls your on-off switch?
- Who has the on-off switches in your class?
- Keep them closed. Keep them open.
- What is it like to have your switch in neutral.
- When were you switched on for the longest period of time? What kinds of people, things, or events switched you on then?
- When were you switched off for the longest period of time? What kinds of people, things or events switched you off then?

more:
- Ask o . . .
  you . . .
  their . . .
- Design . . .
  which . . .
  qualities . . .
- Choose an . . .
  role play . . .
  it makes . . .
  choose. . . .

. . .TE HIGH RISK SITUATIONS. LET IT BE . . . WHATEVER HAPPENS IS RIGHT. . . A VERY HIGH TRUST ENVIRONMENT IS NECESSAR. . .

more:
- Become the role you play for a period, e.g., actually do the principal's thing for a period.
- TEACHER: Play a role of someone and have the kids psych you out.
- How can you tell if someone's role playing? If you are?
- Is role playing necessary in life?
- Does role playing ever become dangerous? When?

Pretend that whales ruled the earth. Write legislation from a whale's point of view that would protect the rights of humans.

Explore the concept of the "melting pot" idea of cultural homogenization and see what's favorable and unfavorable about it.

MAKE A WEB OF LIFE FOR YOUR COMMUNITY.

PLURALASTING . . . CELEBRATING DIVERSITY AS SAMENESS

Plurality is a reality of natural systems. It has been said that only ten percent of all the varieties of living things that ever lived are on the earth today. Multiplicity is the way of nature. In the past there have been cultural tendencies to fragment and isolate rather than to make whole and celebrate. There can be unity in diversity. The following activities can blend these ambiguities:

Create and express Mother Nature's Bill of Rights for all things.

Some Native Americans use the term "long-living" people. Figure out what this means and find a way to celebrate it in your community.

Create a game that little kids and adults can play together using a ball. Make sure the rules are such that everybody feels good and plays hard.

Create slide shows from a collection of throwaway slides someone has collected over the years.

Photograph concepts.

Make a concept picture book

IMMEDIATE . . . SEEING IS BELOVING

Most students in school possess very high degrees of visual competence. As a result, the way most media are used in schools is deficient. For example, most films and filmstrips designed for instruction do exactly what a book does . . . they present ideas in a linear sequence. The potential for visual media is seldom celebrated. Much of this attitude exists because there has never been an attitude toward tolerating ambiguity in education. Linear thought and linear-mindedness are the attitudes that have been accepted. Visual media have a high capacity to nurture inventiveness. Here are some things you can do.

Show films silent and have the students tape a sound track.

Survey your students to find out what T.V. programs they watch . . . Then watch the programs they view for at least one week.

Show films so the sound track alone comes on. Then have the students describe or draw the images.

IF YOU GAINED ANYTHING FROM THE PREVIOUS PAGES OF ACTIVITIES, THIS PAGE WILL BE USEFUL TO YOU. WE DON'T KNOW HOW, , BUT IF YOU WANT TO . . . YOU WILL FIND A WAY!

ASSIGNMENTS

Meadowlark

Take (draw) a picture of secretary power

Develop vocabulary of nonsense words that describe lunch hour; then use the vocabulary to write a poem or essay describing lunch hour.

Have a conversation with the school building (your room) and find out what it thinks of its history, present, and future.

Generate a list of positives that have no negatives. Use only the words on your list to communicate for one hour.

List the ten most important things you know. Underline the ones you learned in a formal educational setting.

Write a song about you and someone who has power over you. Write one about you and someone over whom you have power.

CHECKLISTS

What am I doing here?

What are they doing here?

A semantic differential for faculty meetings

A True-False test for my involvement in school politics

Objective randomization

Safety-Growth

Things I can and can't do

Things I will let other do and things I won't

Reasons things don't happen

Reasons things happen

Carry on or Carrion

Cost and Effect

Be cause

Image a nation

Expect to Rate (I don't give a spit)

These activites and strategies are more than that. *They represent ways to create more*. All of the ESSENCE Materials mentioned earlier were created by classroom teachers. And there is no question in our minds about the competence of any teacher who chooses to create activities designed to nurture WHOLE learning.

Our commitment is to the whole teacher and to the whole child. These activities and strategies we offer you are, as we have said, more biased toward metaphoric mind function. But as we also said at the beginning of this section of the book . . . we offer more metaphoric and synergic mind activities here because most existing instructional materials and strategies are biased toward the rational.

For us the true reward is the celebration of both. That is the way of whole humans. That is the way of WHOLESCHOOLS.

if I fish
and give you
a meal
you will eat for a day...
"if I teach you
to fish
you will eat
all your days!
(a traditional saying)

Visions, Dreams, and Other Realities

Personal Harvests

*"It's funny . . . I 'anoint' them and they go on —
student body president, college political figure,
and some sort of positive activist. One year,
maybe an hour a day, and the rest of their life is
different. I can't dwell on it — I might be
tempted to take it too seriously — but I
remember the impact a couple, maybe three, of
my teachers had on me too."*

Though students are the focus, we have come to believe that the most important single influence on education is the teacher.

Local school boards and parents can have an impact. Building principals can make a difference. Curriculum materials can help. Methods can assist. The shape of the school room and arrangement of the furniture can influence. But all of these things come through one source. YOU.

What you are as a person is vital. You are vital not only to each student, but to yourself as well. Students go away every 181 days or so. *You stay!*

It is romantic and fashionable to say that the students are the most important people in the classroom. But such a statement is either incomplete or dishonest. The teacher is the model. As we have said in the introduction to this book, *teachers have the power.* How they use the power depends on what they are as people. What each teacher is as a person communicates far more than all the assembled curricula, methodologies, equipment, and experiences.

But what each teacher is as a person is a very private thing. We do not want to intrude on your privacy. What we *do* want to do in this section of the book is to provide you with some constructs and some techniques that *you* may use, if you choose, to get more in touch with your psychological style as a teacher — and as a human being.

215

He walked into the class a few weeks late. These were freshmen, but he must have been more than six feet tall — and full — a wistful child in a man's body. But that first day and for weeks after, none of the tenderness showed. He hardly spoke — but wore dark clouds, looking tough, mean, not to be messed with. Soon we discovered that though he could write his name, it was with some effort . . . and sentences were not a possibility. Given standard diagnosis to determine reading level, he tested "preprimer." That is, through one-on-one diagnosis with a compassionate and gentle reading specialist able to take much that was threatening out of the situation, he proved a functional nonreader.

Weeks passed. And then months. It was almost Christmas. Young, single, female teacher getting almost all my sustenance from the school setting, and I decided to leave . . . to get a "national" view . . . to accept a job in another state, involving curriculum work at the national level.

Charlie and I sat on the stairs outside the classroom. All the students knew I was leaving. We were having a party — they'd managed to stage the triumphant "surprise party." Charlie was crying. I was crying. Other students were crying. But it was Charlie and I alone on the stairs for a few moments.

"Are you really going?"
"Yes."
"I don't want you to go."
"Let me know if I can ever do anything . . . I'll come back."

The ache to the depths of my body will never really go. An ache I treasure, for choosing to care so much. An ache I lament without really understanding. He was writing sentences now. And was up to "fifth-grade" reading level.

216

You can't go back. Tom Wolfe said it, "You can't go home again." But you can choose where you'll be . . . and be there.

Sometimes it is with people you have not seen in years, and you feel as if you are picking up the flow of shared communion "midsentence." Sometimes that happens with "students." A letter, a phone call — especially when there is a letter of recommendation due, a job they want.

But those aren't strings. And they aren't my motivation for teaching.

They are — I think — something that goes with seeing the students as the focus for what teaching is all about. The IDEAS are exciting — rich, stimulating, nurturing each of us each day over time. But there would be no webs without spiders to spin them, no honey without bees . . . what we see as the lumber, nails, and glue of our society would take no shape without the carpenters. And the students will be the carpenters.

Can you see that and believe they can build a house without you?

WHAT YOU ARE
SPEAKS SO LOUDLY
PEOPLE CAN'T HEAR
WHAT YOU SAY
WHAT YOU ARE
SPEAKS SO LOUDLY
PEOPLE CAN'T HEAR
WHAT YOU SAY

"HOW CAN YOU KEEP SO CALM WHEN THE WHOLE ROOM IS FALLING APART?!"

Each human being is different from every other. Some people explode at what seems to be nothing. Others could witness the end of the world with expressions of peace on their faces.

Each person has a stress limit that establishes how long and under what conditions she or he can keep "cool." Keeping "cool" is simply being relaxed and comfortable.

A new teacher is often upset when all the students in the class go to the pencil sharpener at once . . . particularly if the first implement sharpened turns out to be a ball point pen.

The same teacher might well remain at ease when a 200-gallon aquarium bursts at the seams.

If an outside observer were to compare the two incidents, it might be hard for that person to understand why the snarled pen represented more of a stress than the broken aquarium. An outside observer can only guess . . . *but the teacher knows.*

stress is a personal thing

For every person in the world, a certain group of things create real stress when they occur. These catalysts to stress are highly personal. The new teacher just mentioned might never become stressed by real catastrophes — but a trivial, pointless kind of event could make him or her furious. As it turned out, the teacher in this case felt the students were bright enough not to make what he considered to be stupid mistakes . . . and thus he became stressed, manifesting the stress by anger, when they did things he felt were beneath them.

This teacher was quick to suppress that anger. And he was also quick to assume responsibility for the anger. Though in this case he considered the mistake stupid . . . *he did not think the students were stupid.* He did, however, feel *he* was stupid to get angry about such trivial things.

The real issue with stress is not the nature of the stress. That is, it is not terribly important to make a list of different kinds of stresses and say that those at the top of the list are the *most* stressful for people and those at the end are the least stressful.

The real issue with stress is where the person believes the stress resides. It is not the *kind* of stress that matters. It is where each person assigns the blame for the stress that really makes the difference.

Most often, people place the blame for the stress either inside themselves or outside. Those who *internalize* the blame for stress are quick to accept the idea that they themselves are to blame for what they choose to allow to stress them.

The other group of people places the responsibility for the stress *outside* themselves. They believe that *others* are responsible for stressing them.

In all of psychology this issue is one of the most hotly contested. One group argues that no one can be responsible for how he or she has been conditioned by others (behaviorists and Freudians). The other group — comprised mostly of the humanists — assigns the majority of the responsibility to the individual. This second group argues that each person is primarily responsible for his or her own stresses.

Of course, both are right and both are wrong.

No one is totally responsible for what he or she is. That is, no one is totally responsible for one's genetic makeup — whether male or female, black or nonblack, mongoloid or normal. These are states of being over which we have little or no control. On the other hand, it is possible to have far more control over what does and does not stress us while realizing at the same time that many people other than ourselves have influenced our ideas, attitudes, and beliefs.

The ways each of us adjust to the resolution of stress and the place we assign responsibility for stress determine our basic, or *core,* personality. Much research has been aimed at determining the kind of personalities that exist and determining if they can change.

A person's core personality differs remarkably from one's overall personality. At least this is the view of O.J. Harvey, the University of Colorado psychologist who has done most of the research in these areas relating to education.

The core personality is the personality that emerges under stress. When people are "cool," it is possible for nearly any kind of posture to emerge. But when stress appears, the psychic survival strategies that each person has chosen will burst forth.

If a person's basic core personality is *extrinsic,* or externally oriented, that person will perceive the sources of stress to be outside the self. Such a person will look to conditions outside the self to focus on — in the environment or within other people.

An *intrinsic,* or inner-focused, person will immediately do a self-check and find out what it is within the self that seems to be stressed by what is happening.

Though this is a simplified way of looking at core personality and stress, it does represent the basic issue.

Whatever a person does to respond to stress is a portrait of that individual's core personality. When there is no stress, most people can play out a whole list of roles — playfully coping with things that come up. Teachers in classrooms gain experience rapidly. Often with several years of experience, they will just smile at something that might bring a surge of panic to a student teacher.

However, this does not mean that the classroom of the experienced teacher, or any teacher, is a stress-free place . . . for the teacher *or* for the students. It is *not.* At least not usually. In fact, teaching ranks high on the list of high-stress professions. Humans who engage in affecting and molding other people's lives are always exposed to stress. When that number of others rises to 25 or 35, an average classroom size for a number of teachers, the stresses are compounded.

There is a delicate zone in which people can cope with compassion and strength. If the stresses become too great, some teachers retreat into an iron-clad shell of rules and authoritative regulations. They resort to the fatal strategy of changing their behavior in ways inconsistent with their motivation. They begin to live a model of basic deception.

This seems as good a time as any to make what may be an obvious AN-NOUNCEMENT:

There is a difference between motivation and behavior.

Motivation is the reason you do something.

Behavior is what you do.

To borrow the old adage, "Things aren't always what they seem." People will often feel one way and act another. I am the only person who has any way of knowing the reason I have done something. Just as you are the only person who can really know your reason for doing something.

I can see your behavior . . . but not your motivation.

Again, people's motivations are not always consistent with their behaviors. To use a convenient example, I might see you seated somewhere reading this book. I might assume that you were reading the book because you were interested in it. I might think by your behavior — the act of reading the book — that your motivation was interest in the book. Your motivation might in fact be that this book appears on *someone's* required reading list.

We mention this because of the awesome amount of energy spent by some teachers in doing and saying things they don't really believe or for some end they think the students won't recognize. That kind of energy spent is unnecessary . . . and besides, it won't work.

Children as young as three years of age can verbalize when some adult in their presence is lying to them. Examples of lies can be promises not intended to be kept, praise that isn't sincere, and reasons offered that don't seem real. An adult's behavior that is not honestly linked to motivation can almost never go undetected by a child. Teachers, unaware of this or not willing to recognize it, can spend much of their time creating unfortunate energy cycles . . . perpetuating a sort of disease of hypocrisy that can, over time, spread to the children.

The teacher *has* the power. The teacher controls. The teacher decides what will be taught, how it will be taught, and how the people taught will be "judged."

Teachers also reach into the home. They affect periods of time that students ordinarily share with their families and friends. Through homework, discussions of the day's events, obvious and more subtle ways, the influence of teachers on the lives of their students is pervasive.

Teachers create an environment of morality and values that their students are forced to experience. Any setting in which a teacher is the instructional leader is laden with that teacher's values. The emotion-wrought question in some communities concerning whether or not teachers *ought* to teach specific values is moot. Teachers *do* teach specific values. And that can't be helped. What *can* be helped is to recognize that they do. Just by recognizing that each teacher's approach to teaching and view of the world affects the students with whom he or she comes in contact is a step toward a more realistic, honest, and humane acknowledgement of the responsibilities involved. In such settings, no specific values are forced on the students. Instead, personal values are allowed to flourish in openness — with each person free to choose and act individually.

Even in these kinds of settings, the teacher *still* has the power. But we'll opt any time for teachers' use of power to extend the options of others. When people are allowed to choose freely from the widest possible array of options, we believe, they will choose what is best for themselves *and* others.

223

To Review . . .

The way a teacher's power is exerted is directly related to his or her core personality. A person's core personality — way of responding to stress — creates a kind of psychological ecology that powerfully influences others who experience it.

This means that what the teacher *is* as a person is probably the single most influential thing in the entire teaching situation. Students, with less power than the teacher, are forced to respond to the teacher. The teacher may or may *not* choose to respond to the students. Again, this depends on the teacher's personality.

What this means, then, is this: If you are a teacher, a controller . . . the most important aspect of your teaching effectiveness is what you are as a person.

Textbooks, laboratory equipment, supplies, and the number of class periods you teach per day are far less influential than simply the person you are.

As weighty as these claims are, they are borne out by research and experience. Adults, when asked about their teachers years after their school experience, are quick to talk about the personalities of the teachers rather than specifically what they learned.

Studies show that try hard as they can, teachers cannot hide their core personalities from any school-age child. Even children as young as three years of age are able to describe the basic stress patterns of all adults who have control over them.

In the next few pages we will explore what we consider to be three basic core personality postures. Of course, there are variations on these — but the three chosen are the dominant types of those identified by researchers. Remember, the examples chosen were all selected to represent *core* personalities. The personality that emerges under stress. Also remember that when a person is under stress, that person's behavior is linked closely to motivation. That is, the person isn't faking it!

AUTHORITARIAN

THE AUTHORITARIAN CORE PERSONALITY

The TRUE BELIEVER. The one who KNOWS what is right and wrong. INFLEXIBLE. If you disagree, you are wrong. If you believe, you are good. If you do not believe, you are bad. Sees the world in two kinds of people: good, smart people who agree . . . bad, stupid people who disagree. You are either with or against this person. Morality and information are closely related. Strong sense of history or future.

TEACHER: (upon finishing a lecture on the Bill of Rights) Well, class . . . there you are — the most noble document that mankind has invented. The document that clearly makes us the one example of a free society on the face of the earth. Any questions?

STUDENT: (looks side to side and then sits up from a slouch to ask the question; he pauses nervously but then asks in a less than assured voice) If that crap is all that great, then why doesn't it apply to us as students?

TEACHER: (icily) MASON . . . Freedom is something extended to those who have the responsibility to *earn* it. Students seem generally capable only of acts of indecency and disrespect. Human values require commitment and discipline — something sadly lacking in most students . . . which, by the way, you have perfectly illustrated.

The true believer knows that any stress that is created is someone else's fault. True believers know this because they see themselves as perfect. If someone disagrees with them, that person is dealt with almost anonymously. For example, the teacher in the anecdote didn't go directly to Mason, but rather to a remote set of values and moral postures. "Responsibility," "commitment," and "discipline" were invoked . . . and "indecency" and "disrespect" were aimed at the student.

Poor Mason doesn't have a chance. The power is immutable and any questioning of the teacher is a questioning of THE TRUTH. An Authoritarian is a strange blend of invulnerability and fragility. Authoritarians see themselves as spokespersons for a higher kind of morality, and yet they are always sensitive to any kind of attack. They don't seem to really believe that their TRUTH — whatever it is — can stand on its own. They always try to wave its banner whenever an "enemy" appears.

Authoritarians are very fragile people, since at some psychic level they know that their whole human investment is in something outside themselves. They have a tendency toward the abuse of power and violence because they somehow believe that the right to use such strategies has been given to them. Authoritarians may be positive or negative in their zeal. Some are very consistent with prevailing social systems and support them as being true — fulfilling their roles as true believers. We usually refer to these simply as Authoritarians. Others, called "revolutionaries" by the dominant system, are just as zealous, but totally against anything representing the "status quo." They invoke authorities, but their authorities are all antiestablishment. We call these negative zealots Antiauthoritarians. Ironically, Authoritarians and Antiauthoritarians share nearly identical personality cores. We think there are actually very few true Authoritarians, either positive or negative, in the United States today.

THE DEPENDENCY CORE PERSONALITY

Wishy Washy. MANIPULATIVE. Always making deals. Trading off. Critical of others or of self. Constantly seeking or giving approval. Believes ways justifies means. Always checking out *other* people's motivations. If you agree, you like me. If you disagree, you hate me. Feels persecuted or spends time persecuting. "If I could make you understand me, you would like me."

TEACHER:	How many of you did your homework like I asked you to? (All hands raise but two.)
	(obviously notices the two) That's fine, class, but how about you, Linda? And what happened to you, Tommy? (Class looks toward the errant two.)
	Nearly all of us did what we were told, didn't we!
CLASS:	(in unison, except for Tommy and Linda) Yes . . . .
TEACHER:	But two of you didn't want to follow directions and do things like you were told. Tommy, Linda . . . would you tell the rest of the class why you chose not to obey your teacher's directions!

DEPENDENCY

The Dependency core personality is a master manipulator. Quite often, such people are unaware that they are being manipulative. However, they are deeply affected by the responses of all the people with whom they have contact. Whereas the Authoritarian's ego strength depends on concepts, ideologies, and abstract belief systems, the Dependency personality is linked directly to people. It is true that when Dependency personalities are under stress, they may invoke concepts, ideologies, and belief systems . . . but their real focus is on the person who represents the stress. Whereas the Authoritarian is often abstract, the Dependency person is always personal.

The Dependency core personality is wracked by insecurities. In a teacher, this ego vulnerability is particularly devastating. To the Dependency core personality, Linda and Tommy didn't just forget their homework; what they did is perceived as an intentional insult to the teacher. They acted *against* the teacher — not the assignment. Such confrontations constantly plague the Dependency person. The whole world seems to be an aggregate of people who either respond or do not respond to the Dependency person's manipulation. For such personality types, stress is nearly always present. They continuously scurry about looking for the violence they perceive the world to be doing to them personally.

DEPENDENCY

The subtle agony of the Dependency core personality is that each of these people receives energy and is drained of energy by people. They spend an inordinate amount of time worrying about what other people think of them. Thus Dependency core personality types are highly vulnerable to any changes in relationships. They set up ground rules and expect them to be followed. If colleagues, students, partners, or even their own children *change* over time, they often feel psychically defeated. Dependency persons may take one of two postures, just as Authoritarian types may. They may be positively oriented toward manipulation and thus manipulate and control others. Or, they may be negatively oriented to manipulation and insist on submitting to the control of others. Some try to perfect both roles at once. Of the three basic core personality types we will present, we think there are more adult Dependency core personality types than either of the other two types. But there is an increasing movement in numbers toward the third core personality type we will describe.

INTRINSIC

THE INTRINSIC CORE PERSONALITY

Self-reliant. TAKES RESPONSIBILITY FOR OWN ACTIONS. Flexible. Open-minded. Different. Not at all pushy. Gets things done. Changes mind freely. FUNNY . . . good sense of humor. Lots of energy. HONEST. Critical but with suggestions. Doesn't get flustered. Lots of good ideas. Seems inventive. Doesn't plan much. Doesn't lay trips on other people. CREATIVE. Playful. UNpredictable.

MALE TEACHER:	I'm going to give you people my view of sexism.
FEMALE STUDENT:	(animatedly) Here come de pig . . . Here come de pig!
	(laughter)
	(pretending to be wounded) I'm not a chauvinist . . . I accept male superiority without being prejudiced against my female "inferiors!"
CLASS:	O o o o o . . . Bro o o o th e e e r!
TEACHER:	(laughing) I know it was a joke, but believe me, the culture has prepared males to believe that kind of stuff. And it happens in many ways.
	(more seriously) Let's explore my sexism, my chauvinism . . . maybe my *adultism* . . . let's explore all my prejudices for a few minutes (more lightly) or as many as we have time for!

230

The Intrinsic core personality has such high ego strength that these people tend to greet nearly all unexpected inputs as positive. To them, failure — or what others tend to consider failure — is simply "positive feedback."

These people are so flexible that no external plan tends to overshadow the immediate things that happen. Interruptions or crises that tend to stress others are seen as fresh breezes on sultry days.

Intrinsic folks tend to become "cooler" as stress increases. They literally seem to feed off crisis energy. As one researcher put it, "They seem to get interested only when the bases are loaded with two outs in the last half of the ninth inning!"

This doesn't mean that Intrinsic people seek out stress. It does mean that when stress does appear, it is greeted with a calm kind of inner strength and competence.

Intrinsic people seldom look outside of themselves when stresses occur. Instead, these people turn *within* and take an introspective look at what they are *letting* bother them. They know they can willfully *choose* whether or not to allow things to stress them.

INTRINSIC

The Intrinsic personality is very strong. Its strength comes in large part from the flexibility it possesses. Unlike the rigid, unyielding Authoritarian, the Intrinsic person recognizes when it is necessary to change. But the Intrinsic person doesn't winnow back and forth just to please others, as do the Dependency types. The best way to sum up the Intrinsic personality is to emphasize that this personality type takes responsibility for its actions.

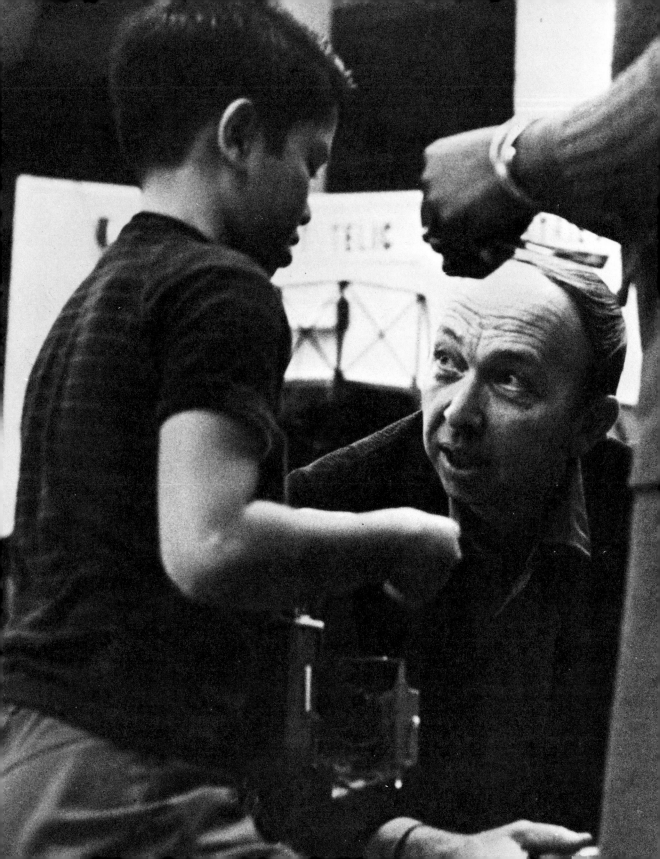

The issues that have been emphasized here are not linked solely to teachers and teaching. These are issues related to the patterns people use when engaged in the process of living life.

Authoritarian and Dependency personality types simply have a higher incidence of mental illness than do Intrinsic people.

Intrinsic people are often highly committed to the things they do. Critics of this posture usually argue that the Intrinsic personality is self-centered and doesn't care about the world and other people. Nothing could be farther from the truth. However, the commitment does differ. Intrinsic people are seldom committed to an idea because they believe they have a vision of the "truth." They are committed because they *want* to be. Likewise, they seldom focus on an idea so as to be able to manipulate others. They resent being manipulated themselves, so they seldom manipulate others.

Once humans accept the responsibility for their own actions, they seldom wander exploitatively among others. Once they have been satisfied that they can control the majority of their own destiny, they do not find it rewarding to manipulate others. Help from such people is far different from the so-called "help" that many give in an effort to control and obligate others.

If there is to be "help" in education, hopefully it will be the guidance, encouragement, and facilitation of learning that comes from a person whose own psychic house is in good order.

Of all the slogans that represent the best in education, perhaps this is one as central to both teaching and learning as any. Or perhaps it is more central to the whole of being:

BECOME THE KIND OF PERSON YOU WANT TO EXPERIENCE.

BECOME THE KIND OF PERSON YOU WANT TO EXPERIENCE

Many fail to realize that each of us can change our core personality. And all of us at some time evidence characteristics of *each* of the core personalities. We all gather psychological habits as we grow up, go to school, and enter adulthood. Each of these habits combines with others and weaves into our strengths and fears and eventually becomes the core personality that guides our lives.

But all habits can be changed. Before a habit can be changed, however, you have to know what it is. The following list of activities first described in a book called OPENING: A PRIMER FOR SELF ACTUALIZATION can help a person become aware of the habits developed to externalize responsibility. Even if you discover through use of these activities that you do externalize responsibility, that does not necessarily mean you are extrinsic or a person who blames everything on everyone else. But each of these activities can give you an idea about how subtle such habits can become and give you some places — without necessarily involving anyone else — to begin to make changes in your psychological habits, if you choose.

...it's *your* turn

INCOUNTER

Check the source of each emotion you feel.

This is a *where* issue, not a what or why. Just figure out if any emotion you feel has its source *inside* you or *outside* you. That is, do you always say, "You make me mad!" or "She makes me feel good!"? If so, at a very subtle level you are externalizing your emotions. *It is a psychological impossibility for an emotion to be outside you!*

Check your tendency to scapegoat.

Scapegoating is the act of blaming someone or something else for what you are doing or believe. It is externalizing responsibility. Extrinsic people do this a lot. It is the favorite pastime of Authoritarian and Dependency core personalities.

Check your tendency to compete.

In spite of what our Darwin-minded vision of people tells us . . . it is basically unnatural to compete. Competition requires "keeping score." This means that when you compete, you are chalking up points. Even in arguments or conversations, people speak of "making a point." Becoming aware of when you do this gives you an idea of how frequently you allow the external to influence what you do.

Check how often you ask questions.

Questions generally put other people on the defensive. They are conversational acts of aggression. Many people do not realize this. They defend questions by saying, "I ask them because I really care." Or, they feel they will sound egocentric if they speak to other people in the form of first-person declarative statements, such as "I think . . . ," rather than initiating conversation, particularly with strangers, by question-asking. We suggest that this dependence on questions is a characteristic of the dominant culture in the United States. We have chosen to show caring and concern through a basically aggressive act. Questions, with their aggression inherent, are not necessarily bad or good between peers. But if there is a power difference between those involved, the aggressor owns the responsibility.

236

Check how often you require others to justify their actions.

The question WHY? is one that requires the person being questioned to justify actions, beliefs, or attitudes. It is not a data-seeking question like WHAT. It is the most aggressive of questions. Even therapists ask questions carefully.

Check how often you ask yourself WHY.

When you ask yourself WHY, it is a request for self-justification. Most people we have talked with say they do this to get a "better understanding of themselves." Yet what we saw them really doing was to invent better excuses for what they did. It became a kind of internalized scapegoating. The real issue was to ask oneself WHAT they did — and if they want to do it again.

Check how compulsively you include others in your plans without their permission.

The quickest way to determine this is to try to speak in the first-person singular for a while. Often people do not realize that when they say "WE" instead of "I," they expect others to be ready to go along with their plans. Teachers are awesomely guilty of being spokespersons for the whole class by saying things like, "Now we all want to be quiet, don't we."

Check how continuously you evaluate and judge others.

One of the most stressful situations for people to be in is one in which all that they do is being judged. Strangely, our language lends itself to patterns of communication that are highly judgmentative. We constantly comment on such things, for example, as "That's a beautiful sunset," "I like cats but can't stand dogs," or "I hate that music." What many people do not realize is that if my speech is full of such judgments, children or any other people in my presence will begin to suspect that they too are being judged.

Now the purpose of these "checks" is not to communicate a life-style or a set of rules to live by. Rather, the intent is to give you some way to develop an awareness of the "habits" that may have formed in your psyche. After you have developed this heightened awareness, you can decide whether or not you want to make any changes. Changes you make like this are an exercise of your will.

It is by exercising such choices we have seen hundreds of people move toward more Intrinsic personality postures. Intrinsic people, as we have said before, simply have a higher level of mental health than others do. They are closer to what Abraham Maslow has called self-actualization. As teachers, they tend to create healthier and more effective learning environments.

14

Meadows of Love

To teach is to express Love...

Love.

Love? . . . of what? of whom?

Each human is an expression of love. Sometimes a bitter, withered expression . . . one born of frustration and failure. Sometimes slightly withheld, tentative, and cautious. And sometimes an absolutely triumphant explosion of love that pours as a stream into everyone's presence.

For some, their love is linked to what they know . . . to others, how they know it.

Some love who they know and how they know them. Some love power and control. Some love submission and nonresistance.

Whatever it is that we love, there is no love more stable than one's love of self.

True love . . . of self.

. . . but?

Doesn't a love of self mean *selfish*? Doesn't it mean exploitation? Can I love myself *and* love others? Can I love others without loving myself?

All of these issues are related to the basic view one has about the human condition. Earlier we claimed that love is synergic. That is, it always contains more than can be accounted for. Love *is* a human expression of synergy. But to look at the role of self in loving produces some remarkable ways of knowing about teaching, living, and the wholeness of being human.

The *selfish* human is an exploiter of others . . . of the outside. Such people brutalize the external to fill up the gnawing void they see within their own souls. They cannot love themselves, because as hard as they try, they can never take enough from the outside to fill up what they will not let themselves become.

The *selfless* person is an exploiter of self . . . of themselves. Such people brutalize themselves to try to make their emptiness legitimate. They cannot stop giving long enough to love themselves. They presume others to be as inadequate as they and are compelled to express their empty vision of love by filling cups that have not been offered.

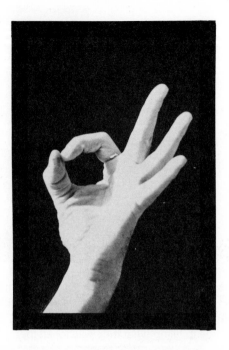

To love one's self, one must both give and receive. And one must give and receive with the knowledge that the basic motivation is to celebrate and not to exploit.

It is at this point that we come again to the primal context of motivation. Love of self requires an equilibrium of motivation to give and to receive. It is only in this context that one can truly teach what one intends to teach.

The person with *selfness* is a person who celebrates. Such people love themselves enough to know they must receive to be able to give, and they are continuously transformed by these acts. They give freely, knowing they will receive when it is time.

In the classroom, as in all of the rooms of our lives, the love of one's self carries with it the degree of honesty that makes it possible for motivation and behavior to be genuinely linked. Students of any age are quick to hear the person who says, "I love you," and means, "Do as I say — I am going to get a few year's experience and go into administration." They also hear the person who says, "I love you," and means, "I am doing this job just to get enough money to put my partner through graduate school." And one that never goes undetected is the voice that says, "I love you," and means, "I am the bearer of truth and I am here to convert you."

Equally detectable is the person who comes to students and says, "I love you," and means, "I am inadequate, nobody needs me, so I am going to see if I can make you need me."

The teacher who says, "I love you," and means, "I love you and I love me," is also recognizable. Though this posture may take a bit longer for the students to recognize, they will. It takes longer because it is more rare in the students' experience.

OH THAT I COULD
TEACH IN A WAY
TO CELEBRATE US BOTH . . .
I WOULD
NEVER GIVE YOU A TASK
AND CALL IT HONORABLE
UNLESS IT COULD ADD
TO YOUR BEING.

If people are honest, love themselves, and their motivation is directly linked to their behavior . . . they teach far more of worth than those things identified simply as the "curriculum." They teach themselves as an image of humanness that their students can touch and find real.

When such a teacher comes to a student and says, "That's really good!" the student knows that the teacher actually thinks it is good. But because the student is likely to have experienced many adults who have lied in the name of such educational strategies as *positive reinforcement*, the student will know the difference. To be told that one has performed well or has pleased an authority figure, when in fact one has not, is nearly always recognizable to a student. What students learn in such settings is how well they accommodate to deceit. They also learn what the teacher really thinks of them. They learn to know how much the teacher thinks it takes to buy them off. But the tragedy of such actions is even more pervasive.

If the students are at all insecure, they might believe that the teacher actually knows something they don't. Students finding themselves in such situations can come to believe that they are capable of performing only at a trivial level.

At about the fourth-grade level, many minority children in large, urban school settings seem to lose hope and effectively "drop out" of the school experience. Many of the black educators and psychologists with whom we have worked have criticized schools and teachers for having given up on the students at this level. They argue that more attention should be exerted, more force, and, if necessary, more discipline.

We would argue that what is needed is . . . more *honesty*! Dominant-culture school practices may well have nurtured settings of deceit on the basis of creating settings of compassion. Giving better grades to someone who doesn't deserve them is a poor substitute for honesty. It keeps children looking outward for rewards while they learn to internalize a tolerance for deceit. Such acts create a psychic time bomb destined to explode at an undetermined time.

When
I am strong enough
to see myself clearly
and accept responsibility
for my actions
I am strong enough
to honestly
let others
grow
and change
in my presence.

Seasons of Synergy
15

There is much to the particle of the universe called humankind. Our cultural journey has given us many messages. We have heard how things have been and how they could be. We have seen a vision of humankind described on the basis of its faults, its inadequacies, and its deficiencies. We are seeing now the emergence of a newer, perhaps truer vision of humankind. A vision that embodies hope, goodness, aspiration, and perhaps a transcendence of ways of knowing that confine the human spirit.

Cultural critics often argue that for us to solve the problems of the present, we must reapply the solutions of the past. We must, they argue, return to the methodologies of logic, of reason, and of rationality. Yet these same critics find it difficult to admit that the current issues facing humankind may well be the result of having applied those methodologies of linearity in the past.

We feel that we are at a point in the history of humankind where logic, reason, and rationality must be revitalized, reenriched, and if you will go along still with our image of gardens . . . refertilized, organically! This is the time to pay as much attention to metaphor, to intuition, and to a cyclical kind of knowing as we do to our well-practiced linear skills. By paying attention to both intuition and reason . . . by seeing cycles as well as lines . . . we can nurture a holistic kind of knowing, and the transformative mind may emerge.

In the preceding pages, we have chosen to share our perceptions about where we are at this stage of the art. These have been our perceptions, and we claim honesty but make no pretense at knowing the "truth." We have chosen to present information and opinions in ways different from those you can usually find these same subjects covered in other places. We have chosen some subjects that tend not to be discussed at all in written form in other places. This has been, in effect, our teaching strategy . . . our own attempt at nurturing transformative thought.

Each of the subjects we have explored here has been a part of our lives. We have included excerpts from our own journals and recollections of our own experiences. The theory and practices we offer include a distillation of our learnings from hundreds of others, repatterned into our own images and words. These pages thus document our own growth.

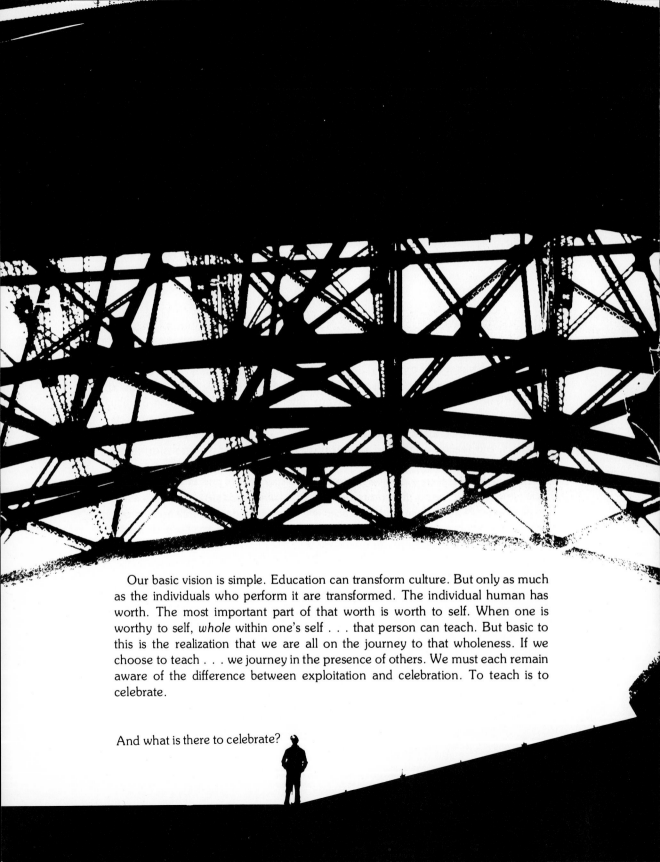

Our basic vision is simple. Education can transform culture. But only as much as the individuals who perform it are transformed. The individual human has worth. The most important part of that worth is worth to self. When one is worthy to self, *whole* within one's self . . . that person can teach. But basic to this is the realization that we are all on the journey to that wholeness. If we choose to teach . . . we journey in the presence of others. We must each remain aware of the difference between exploitation and celebration. To teach is to celebrate.

And what is there to celebrate?

By now it should be clear. Transformation of the culture can take place only to the degree that individuals within it are transformed. Cultures, societies, all of humankind, in fact, is little more than an aggregate of individuals. In the past within the United States, individuals have experienced schooling based on the premise that certain specific and limiting roles and ways of knowing are necessary.

Today's world challenges such premises. Americans who once thought that Saudi Arabia is where Lawrence came from and Rudolf Valentino played are now changing vacation plans and household budgets because of the cost of fuel oil. Affluent nations turn on their color television sets to see starving people in the Third World. Native Americans are winning claims from centuries-old broken treaties. The world *has* become a global village.

For the first time in history, humankind is recognizing the reality of the global village. Decisions made in the chambers of people whose language we cannot read are affecting our lives. The barriers that separate humans are rapidly eroding. Traditions of separation, of isolation, and of social strata are beginning to change. Sexism, racism, adultism, and ageism are now topics of situation comedies on daily television shows. In America, it seems, we have begun to broadcast our fears . . . with the net effect being a greater number of people able to view their fears made public, though with some discomfort. As the discomfort mounts, the potential is there to join in a cleansing rebirth.

Schools are hard put to keep up. At a time when crucial social issues are still touchy topics for most curricula, students can switch the channels of the major television networks and see any or all of these issues portrayed, either as live news or in scriptwriters' fancy. Schools are the only "required course" in our culture, save prisons. They coexist with network television — and each night network TV hangs a portrait of our culture before the viewers' eyes in sharp contrast with school curricula. This disparity gets harder and harder to explain.

The transformation is being accelerated by the growing confrontation between human growth and the capacity nature has to support that growth. It is being exaggerated by social inequities. It is being communicated by the instantaneous command of electronic media.

But more than these things, the transformation is being quietly but insistently demanded. It is demanded by the persistent pulse within each human. It is this pulse that links humans to the source of all things . . . *nature. Transformation and rebirth are the ways of nature.*

Throughout this book we have used examples from nature. We have chosen metaphors from nature to give life to our ideas. Metaphors of garden and meadow and growing things are intentional. George Leonard says it in a film we have made, "nature . . . just communing with nature . . . a traditional and eternally new way of transformation."

Beyond communing, we are talking about reawakening a daily, moment-to-moment sense in all of us . . . reminding us that nature *is* the source. Our good health — emotional, intellectual, physical, spiritual — depends on the good health of planet Earth. All of us as teachers — no matter what our subject-area specialties — can nurture through the activities we choose, the materials we use, and the experiences we provide . . . can nurture this sense of oneness and harmony with all living things.

Human concerns *are* extending to other species and to the planet itself. The survival of whales, oceanic pollution, and the effect of ozone in the atmosphere are commonplace issues in daily conversations. Spirituality is on the rise. New ways of human affiliation are being explored at the same time ancient and traditional ways are being renewed.

What, then, is the role of education? Is it the way for the world to be saved? Probably not. It is unlikely that education can either save or destroy the world. But what it can be is a model of human freedom and dignity. It can be the womb of humanism. The whole minds of teacher and learner can be nourished and celebrated. The schools can become places where all the human qualities — intellectuality, emotionality, and sexuality — can blend into a lasting spiritual experience. The schools can become sites of the true rites of passage. Not passage into habit-worn, routinized experience. But rather passage into a vision of transformation. A vision that will celebrate the human condition rather than exploit it. A vision that will lead us into lasting harmony with nature.

But for all this is a revolution needed? Hardly. Revolution is the way of history. It is a poor tool for current and future politics. A transformed and visionary person is a whole person. There are people like that teaching right now. There have been in the past. The transformation is under way. The choice for our own role in this quiet, urgent celebration belongs to each of us.

WHAT I AM
IS WHAT I TEACH.
WHAT I LOVE
GUIDES THE CELEBRATION.

I CAN LOVE THE MYSTERIES
OF NATURE
I CAN LOVE THE JOURNEYS
OF HUMANKIND

I CAN LOVE THE ORDER
AND CAPRICE OF MIND

I CAN LOVE YOU

BUT TO CONCEIVE
AND GIVE BIRTH
TO ANY OF THESE

I MUST LOVE ME.

Notes to Me

a decidedly irreverent Glossary

Access mode: anything-goes education
Accountability: justification
Ambiguity: almost thinking
Antiauthoritarian: a person bent on destroying the status quo
Assumptions: filters through which we experience life
Auras: energy fields around living things
Authoritarian: a person who protects the status quo
Basics, the: a place education has never been
Behavior: something your motivation makes you do
Behaviorism: a philosophy that exaggerates the importance of behavior
Behaviorists: people who watch other people do things and explain what they
 did
Bruner, Jerome: a psychologist who thinks people know a lot
Centering: getting to the middle of being
Classroom: all of the below and more . . .
  conventional four walls, self-contained: learning box
  four walls, everyone migrates box that flushes
  four walls, student migration: the herd shot round the school
  no walls, street learning approach: legitimate drop-outs
  open space: a place where teachers often have to build walls
  seductive classroom: a place where you would go even if you didn't have to
Cognitive psychology: a philosophy that focuses on intellectual development
Common sense: what keeps us alive
Competition: a human game that has been blamed on the animals
Consciousness: any knowing whether you know it or not
Constancy, object: when you know something is there even if you cannot see it
Core personalities: where you go as last resort when someone threatens your
 psyche
Creativity: new know

264

Dependency core personality: drain brain psyche
Delivery mode: limited learning education
Didactic mode: telling it *the way* it is
Dreams: another kind of reality
Dualism: what is often mislabeled, *dichotomy*
Environment: what hangs around you
Evaluation: a value judgment happening
Evaluweighting: a heavy trip
External environment: out there
Extrinsic: something from out there
Extrinsic core personality: a person held together by out there
First force psychology: heavy Freuday
Fourth force psychology: psychology on both sides of the skin
Freud: a psychologist who cleaned out the basement of the human psyche
Genius: someone who does something very much better than you know how to
    do it
Global village: a McLuhan-y tune
Grades: imaginary boxes
Harvey, O.J.: a psychologist who studies personality under stress
Hemisphere, left cerebral: where most people work
Hemisphere, right cerebral: where most people play
History, natural: what the planet does to us
History, cultural: what we do to the planet
Humanistic psychology: a philosophy that believes people are real
Humor, sense of: something funny
Integrative mode: moving into learning
Interruptions: life's continuity
Intrinsic: something from inner space
Intrinsic core personality: a personality held together by inner space
Inventive mode: new do
I.Q. tests: tests that generally evaluate your symbol mindedness
Learning censor: shape up thinking
Learning poet: ship out thinking
Lesson plans: instructional museums
Logic: the game
Logical thinking: playing the game
Metaphor: restless identities
Metaphoric mind: transformative thinking
Metaphoric modes: ways to transform restless thinking
Method, scientific: what you say you did after you *really* do it
Mind: whatever it wants to be
Mind meadows: places where the mind rolls in the hay
Motivation: behavior's mother

Myth of objectivity: what computers believe in
Objectives: targets
Personality: the way you do life
Piagetian developmental modes: rungs on the ladder of logic
Play: OK.
Positive reinforcement: coercion with a smile
Randomization: entropy thinking
Rationality: thought that fits
Rational modes: ways of fitting
Rational thought: thinking fit
Report cards: rationality's valentines
Rigidity: closed shop thought
Self actualization: living your own game plans
Selfishness: life's coffee cup
Selflessness: life's coffee pot
Selfness: life's coffee tree
Sense of humor: knowing the biggest joke of all is serious
Senses: what gives the world to you
Silence: the thing you do while dreaming
Stress: a razor blade in your psyche
Subject matter exams: instant replay history
Symbolic visual mode: ideasight
Synergy: mystery fits
Synergic comparative mode: blend think
Synergic modes: psychic gardening
Therapy: education done late
Third force psychology: a philosophy of psychology that doesn't pretend people
    are pigeons
Three R's: an abbreviation of one properly and two improperly spelled words
Transformation: a psychic quantum leap
Transformative mind: a mind that knows it can think new
Transformative thought: thinking new
Transpersonal psychology: a philosophy of psychology that believes the human
    psyche extends on both sides of the skin
True believer: a THE WAY zealot
Truth: job security for zealots
Values: prejudices that people like
Vibes: what we didn't know we could know
Visual competence: lookin' good
Whole child: raw material for cultural surgery
Whole human: something that survives cultural surgery

Resources

Abruscato, Joe and Jack Hassard, *Loving and Beyond,* Goodyear, Pacific Palisades, 1976.

Arguelles, Jose A. *The Transformative Vision.* Shambhala, Berkeley, 1975.

Arnheim, Rudolf. *Visual Thinking.* University of California, Berkeley, 1969.

Assagioli, Roberto. *The Act of Will.* Viking, New York, 1973.

Bateson, Gregory. *Steps to an Ecology of Mind.* Ballantine, New York, 1972.

Borton, Terry. *Reach, Touch and Teach.* McGraw Hill, New York, 1970.

Brown, Barbara. *New Mind, New Body,* Harper & Row, New York, 1974.

Bruner, Jerome. *On Knowing: Essays for the Left Hand.* Atheneum, New York, 1962.

Caney, Steven. *Play Book.* Workman, New York, 1975.

Caney, Steven. *Toy Book.* Workman, New York, 1972.

Charles, Cheryl and Ronald Stadsklev, eds. *Learning with Games.* Social Science Education Consortium, Boulder, 1973.

deBono, Edward. *The Mechanism of Mind.* Penguin, Middlesex, 1969.

DeVito, Alfred and Gerald H. Krockover. *Creative Sciencing.* Little Brown, Boston, 1976.

Fabun, Don. *Three Roads to Awareness.* Glencoe, Beverly Hills, 1970.

Faraday, Ann. *Dream Power.* Conward, McCann and Geogheyan, New York, 1972.

Ferguson, Marilyn. *The Brain Revolution.* Taplinger, New York, 1973.

Garfield, Patricia. *Creative Dreaming.* Simon and Schuster, New York, 1974.

Gordon, W.J.J. *Synectics.* Harper and Row, New York, 1961.

Gordon, W.J.J. et al. *The Metaphorical Way.* Porpoise, Cambridge, Mass., 1971.

Hall, Edward. *Beyond Culture.* Doubleday, Garden City, 1976.

Hendricks, Gay and Russel Wills. *The Centering Book.* Prentice Hall, Englewood Cliffs, N.J., 1975.

Illich, Ivan. *Tools for Conviviality*. Harper & Row, New York, 1973.

Jones, Richard M. *Fantasy and Feeling in Education*. Harper & Row, New York, 1968.

Koberg, Don and Jim Bagnall. *The Universal Traveler: A Soft Systems Guide to Creativity, Problem Solving, and the Process of Reaching Goals*. W. Kaufmann, 1974.

Koestler, Arthur. *The Act of Creation*. Macmillan, New York, 1964.

Kubie, Lawrence S. *Neurotic Distortion of the Creative Process*. Noonday, New York, 1958.

Leonard, George. *The Transformation*. Delacorte, New York, 1972.

Leonard, George. *The Ultimate Athlete*. Viking, New York, 1975.

Lipman, Jean. *Provocative Parallels*. Dutton, New York, 1975.

Maslow, Abraham H. *The Psychology of Science*. Regnery, Chicago. 1969.

Maslow, Abraham H. *The Farther Reaches of Human Nature*. Viking, New York, 1971.

Masters, Robert and Jean Houston. *Mind Games*. Dell. New York, 1972.

May, Rollo. *The Courage to Create*. Norton, New York, 1975.

Morman, Jean Mary. *Wonder Under Your Feet*. Harper & Row, New York, 1973.

McKim, Robert. *Experiences in Visual Thinking*. Brooks Cole, Monterey, 1972.

McLuhan, Marshall. *Understanding Media*. New American Library, New York, 1964.

McLuhan, Marshall. *Culture Is Our Business*. Ballantine, New York, 1970.

McLuhan, Marshall. *From Cliche to Archetype*. Pocket Books, New York, 1971.

Ornstein, Robert E. *The Psychology of Consciousness*. Viking, New York, 1972.

Pearce, Joseph Chilton. *The Crack in the Cosmic Egg*. Pocket Books, New York, 1973.

Pearce, Joseph Chilton. *The Magical Child*. Dutton, New York, 1977.

Romey, Bill. *Consciousness and Creativity*. Ash Lad Press, Canton, New York, 1975.

Roszak, Theodore. *Unfinished Animal*. Harper & Row, New York, 1975.

Salk, Jonas. *Man Unfolding*. Harper & Row, New York, 1971.

Samples, Bob and Bob Wohlford. *Opening*. Addison Wesley, Reading, Mass., 1975.

Samples, Bob. *The Metaphoric Mind*. Addison Wesley, Reading, Mass., 1976.

Schrag, Peter and Diane Divoky. *The Myth of the Hyperactive Child*. Pantheon, New York, 1975.

Sheehy, Gail. *Passages*. Dutton, New York, 1976.

Tart, Charles. *Altered States of Consciousness*. Doubleday, Garden City, 1972.

Watts, Alan. *Tao: The Watercourse Way*. Pantheon, New York, 1975.

Watzlawick, Paul et al. *Pragmatics of Human Communication*. Norton, New York, 1967.

Wilson, Colin. *New Pathways of Psychology*. Taplinger, New York, 1972.

This list of resources is in no way intended to be complete. Even some of our favorites are not included here! Knowing its limitations, we still offer this list to you as a beginning. View it as a sharing of our perspective of books that have helped . . . and add your own personal favorites.

Index

Abstract reasoning, 33-35, 48, 187, 229
Access mode, 164-181, 184
Accountability, 8, 60-62
Achievement tests, 7
Ambiguity, 45, 60, 186, 208
Antiauthoritarian, 226-227
Assignment, 1-11, 201, 229
Assumptions, 13, 33, 64, 147
Athletic facilities, 90, 109, 128
Attendance, 67, 94, 141, 146
Attitude inventories, 158
Auras, 20, 41
Authoritarian, 226-227, 229, 231, 233, 236

Basics, the, 3
Behavior, 28-31, 33, 37-38, 56, 58, 218, 221-222, 224, 245, 247
Behaviorism, 24, 28-31, 37-38, 44-45, 56, 58, 220
Behaviorists, 24, 26, 28-31, 37, 44-45, 56, 58, 220
Behavior modification, 30
Book smart, 17
Bricoleur, 203
Bridgeman, Percy, 7
Bruner, Jerome, 18, 33-35

Censor, Learning, 60-71, 73, 87, 194
Classroom, 112-135
   conventional four walls, self-contained, 119-121, 124, 132-134
   four walls, everyone migrates, 128-129, 132-134
   four walls, student migration, 126-127, 132-134
   no walls, street learning approach, 130-131, 132-134
   open space, 122-125, 132-134
   seductive, 118, 132-134
Cognitive psychology, 24, 33-35, 38, 44-45, 56, 58, 184, 220
Common sense, 1-11
Community involvement, 98, 124, 201, 204-205, 223
Competence, 14-21, 30, 38, 94, 124, 172-173, 203, 231
Competition, 170, 172-173, 178, 236
Consciousness, 23, 52, 56, 58, 166
Constancy, object, 33
Contexts, 56, 61
Copernicus, 42
Core personalities, 221-239
   authoritarian, 226-227, 229, 231, 233, 236
   dependency, 228-229, 231, 233, 236
   intrinsic, 230-231, 233
Corpus callosum, 52
Cosby, Bill, 18
Creativity, 17-19, 34, 37, 41, 49, 62, 94, 179, 188-189, 194-195, 197
Culture, 7, 10, 16-17, 23, 30, 34, 52, 60, 67, 73, 98, 101, 154, 157, 165,
     168, 172, 181, 207, 236, 248, 254-255
Custodian, 10, 14, 94, 105

Darwin, Charles, 25, 236
Dependency core personality, 228-229, 231, 233, 236
Delivery mode, 164-181, 184
Dewey, John, 6-7, 10
Diagnostic tools, 155, 158, 216
Dichotomy, 30, 56, 57, 60-71, 95
Didactic mode, 164-181
Diversity, 207
Dreams, 20, 41, 63
Dualism, 56, 62, 68, 71

Ecology, 1, 18, 118, 139, 172, 224
Elephant, 24
Emotion, 1, 3, 10, 13, 30, 37-38, 41, 236, 257
Emotionality, 38, 258
Energy, 17
Erikson, Erik, 26
ESSENCE I and II, 204-205, 210
Evaluation, 38, 63, 87, 94, 154-162, 168, 174-175, 184-185, 188-189, 201, 237
Evaluweighting, 154
Evaluating/evaluloving, 155
Extrinsic, 178, 220-239
Extrinsic core personality, 221-239

First force psychology, 24-27, 38
Flexibility, 14-21, 42, 152, 172, 231
Fourth force psychology, 41-43
Freud, 24-27, 37-38, 44-45, 56, 220

Galileo, 42
Genius, 17-18, 25, 42
Global village, 255
Grades, 155, 156-161

Harvey, O.J., 221
Hemisphere, 47-53
Hemisphere, left cerebral, 48-50, 52-53, 87
Hemisphere, right cerebral, 49, 51-53
Hiding places, 110
History, natural, 148
Holistic, 34, 184
Holistic learning, 184, 252
Homework, 153, 223, 228
Honesty, 13, 142, 154, 160, 162, 223, 230-231, 245, 247-249, 253
Humanism, 24, 37-39, 258
Humanistic psychology, 24, 37-39, 44-45, 56, 58, 220
Humor, sense of, 14-21, 98, 162, 172, 230-231

Imagery, guided, 74-75, 187-189, 198
Inquiry method, 171
Integrative, 51, 184-185, 192
Intellectuality, 38, 258
Intrinsic, 30, 166, 178, 220-239
Intrinsic core personality, 230-231, 233
Intuition, 1-11, 41, 49, 51, 52, 56, 60, 150, 252

Inventive, 49, 51-52, 61, 67, 159, 173, 184-185, 194-195, 196, 203, 208, 229-230, 237, 252
I.Q. tests, 7

Jones, Richard M., 26, 63
Junk, 202

Kirilian photography, 40
Kohl, Herb, 152

L's, three, 68
Learning Censor, 60-71, 73, 87, 194
Learning Poet, 60-71, 73, 194
Lesson plans, 13, 14, 60-61, 152
Linearity, 1-11, 33-35, 48-50, 52, 68, 184-185, 208, 252
Logic, 1-11, 20, 30, 33-35, 42, 48-50, 52, 58, 60, 63, 68, 87, 184-185, 187, 252
Logical modes, 33-35, 48-50, 184-185, 252
Logical thinking, 1-11, 33-35, 48-50
Lounges, 108, 141, 147

Maslow, Abraham, 37-39, 238
Meadow masters, 22-45, 48, 56
Metaphor, 10, 30, 49, 52, 63, 65, 184-185, 189, 198-201, 252, 257
Metaphoric mind, 10, 49, 51-53, 71, 182-213, 210, 252
Metaphoric modes, 49, 51, 182-213, 252
Metaphoric thought, 1-11, 18, 49, 51, 87, 182-213, 252
Method, scientific, 6-7
Mind, 1-11, 17, 23, 52, 56, 63, 71, 94, 155
Mind meadows, 1-11, 17, 20, 23, 46-53, 68, 188
Motivation, 10, 217, 221-222, 224, 228, 245, 247
Multisensory involvement, 42
Myth of objectivity, 8-9

Nasrudin, 54, 56, 70, 86, 97, 99
Natural history, 148
Nature, 23, 183, 256-261
Newton, Isaac, 42

Object constancy, 33
Objectives, 148-151, 152, 184-185
Objectivity, 8-9, 157, 184-185

Parents, 10, 14, 94, 108, 117, 132-133, 141, 143, 153, 155, 157-158, 160, 202, 215, 223
Personality, 7, 16-17, 60, 214-239

273

Personality, core, 221-239
  authoritarian, 226-227, 229, 231, 233, 236
  dependency, 228-229, 231, 233, 236
  intrinsic. 230-231. 233
Philosophy, 6, 22-45, 56, 58, 154, 164-181
Piaget, Jean, 33-35, 37-38, 48, 50, 184
Piagetian developmental modes, 33-35, 48, 50
  formal, 50
  operational, 50
  preoperational, 50
  sensorimotor, 50
Poet, Learning, 60-71, 73, 194
Positive reinforcement, 247
Probability, 8-9
Process mode, 164-181
Psychology, 22-45, 52, 56, 58, 164-181, 220, 214-239, 248
  behavioral, 24, 28-31, 44-45, 56, 58, 220
  cognitive, 24, 33-35, 38, 44-45, 56, 58, 184
  Freudian, 24-27, 37-38, 44-45, 56, 58, 220
  humanistic, 24, 37-39, 44-45, 56, 58, 220
  transpersonal, 24, 41-43, 44-45, 56, 58
  first force, 24-27, 38
  fourth force, 41-43
  second force, 28-31, 38
  third force, 37-39
Puritan ethic, 26, 166, 168-169

Questions, 168, 172, 236, 237

R's, three, 3, 10, 48, 68
Randomization, 196-197
Rationality, 1-11, 33-35, 48-50, 52, 56, 71, 184-185, 196, 210, 252
Rational modes, 33-35, 48-50, 184-185, 196, 252
Rational thought, 18, 33-35, 48-50,   71, 184-185, 196, 210, 252
Reason, 10, 33-35, 252
Reich, Charles, 166
Report cards, 160
Rickles, Don, 18
Rigidity, 16
Rogers, Carl, 37-39
Rokeach, Milton, 16

Scientific method, 6-7
Second force psychology, 28-31, 38

274

Secretary, 104
Self actualization, 37-39, 238
Selfishness, 240-250
Selflessness, 240-250
Selfness, 240-250
Sense of humor, 14-21, 98, 162, 172, 230-231
Senses, 42
Sexuality, 38, 258
Skinner, Burrhus Frederick, 28-31, 37-38
Sputnik, 170
Stimulus, 28-31, 48, 56, 58
Street smart, 3, 10, 17, 20
Stress, 142-144, 154, 214-239
Subject matter exams, 159
Sufi, 52, 54, 62, 70
Surprise, effective, 18
Symbolic Visual, 51, 184-185, 187-189
Synergy, 173, 178-179, 184-185, 190, 196-211, 242
Synergic, 34, 178-179, 184-185, 190, 196-211, 242
Synergic Comparative, 51, 184-185, 190
Synergic modes, 178-179, 184-185, 190, 196-211
Synergic thinking, 34, 178-179, 184-185, 190, 196-211

Third force psychology, 37-39
Three L's, 68
Three R's, 3, 10, 48, 68
Transactional Analysis, 142
Transformation, 47, 60, 98, 250-261
Transformative mind, 252
Transformative thought, 252-253
Transpersonal psychology, 24, 41-43, 44-45, 56, 58
True believer, 169, 226-227
Truth, 7, 168, 178, 181, 227, 233, 253

Values, 16-17, 22-45, 58, 68-69, 94, 98, 223, 226-227
Vibes, 41
Village, global, 255
Visual competence, 49, 184-185, 187-189, 208

Whole child, 210, 250-261
Whole human, 37, 210, 214-239, 242, 250-261
Whole learning, 210, 250-261
Whole mind, 210, 250-261
Whole school, 250-261
Whole teacher, 210, 214-239, 250-261

Thanks

The primary thanks for books must go to those who contributed most in their writing. *THE WHOLESCHOOL BOOK* was primarily created by several tens of thousands of students that we have experienced over the years. They acted out the drama of their own lives in our presence . . . we just wrote down what we were able to see.

Among our own meadow masters were Jerome Bruner, Richard Jones, O.J. Harvey, Carl Rogers, Jonas Salk, David and Frances Hawkins, Eleanor Duckworth, Frances Clark, Lois Knowles, Nina Menrath, Joseph Chilton Pearce, Sidney and Toni Jourard, Rollo May, John Vasconcellos, John Levy, Irving Morrissett, John Thompson, Bill Romey, Gail Griffith Lyons, Harold Stonehouse, Bob Sluss, Ed Kormondy, Willi Unsoeld, Bill Hammond, Matt Brennan, Fred Fox, Jake Nice, David Kennedy, Tony Angell, Barbara Yamamoto, Roy Takayama, Betty Joy, Michele Hensill, Don Covey, Sara Moss Phillips, T. Frank Saunders, Dorothy Sherman, Mary Lou McWilliams, Rodger Bybee, Fred Hanley, Ken Ashley, John O'Connell, John Black, Larry Watts, Victor Barraza, Mary Guptill, Harold Pratt, Martha McGeorge Hunter, Jeanne Bowles McCall, Dorothy Curtis, Bruce Viggars, Evans Clinchey, Jim Davis, Merle Knight, Charles Weingartener, Jim Gladson, Jack Carter, Harold Anderson, Ron Anderson, Jim Wailes, Ken Peterson, Ed Walker, Frank Watson, Millie Loeb, Bob Lepper, Bob Wohlford, Jim McGrath, Michael Hartoonian, Jim Eckenrod, Ted Kaltsounis, Jim Shaver, Howard Mehlinger, Peter Dow, Charles Billings, Larry Senesh, Ron Ridenhour, Richard Brown, Mary Budd Rowe, Emily Girault, Gerry Kelly, Dick Gilbert, Irene and Bill Shelver, Tom and Frances Charles, Eve and Gene Thrall, Perl and Mattie Charles, Phyllis Charles and the other aunts, uncles and cousins, Nick and Suzie Helburn, Fred Risinger, Kathleen Neary Henze, Tom Roberts, Larry Rose, Craig Kissock, Roger and Nancy Wangen, Sam Ramirez, Nick Carter, Nelson Haggerson, Stan Scoville, Tom Henze, and Jim O'Grady.

276

As long as this list is, it is far from complete. But special warmth must go to Ken Peterson, Ed Walker, Frank Watson and Millie Loeb for reading and criticizing this manuscript. The authors assume full responsibility for ignoring many of their wise recommendations. Jan Rensel and Olina Gilbert added their magic in many ways as these pages were born.

On a more personal vein, thanks are due the immediate families involved. Thus Bob and Cheryl grin at each other as well as Stician, their two-year-old, who offered numerous unsolicited and appropriate comments about every facet of this effort. To Rosemary Barnhart and the four other Barnharts, Karyn, Malia, Alyse, and Ronald, we all owe much.

The *Pacific Sun* of Mill Valley, California again showed their skill and grace in the typesetting of this manuscript. Lorna Cunkle and Kathy Parker guided the effort.

The Sufi stories included in this book were adapted and inspired by the work of Idries Shah. See *The Way of the Sufi*, E.P. Dutton and Co., New York, 1970, and other works by Shah for more insight into this oral and philosophical tradition.

73